W9-ABG-399

*Garland Publishing, Inc.*

The chart on page 103 should appear after the text on page 108. Garland Publishing regrets the error in the original printing.

# Literary Impressionism in Jean Rhys, Ford Madox Ford, Joseph Conrad, and Charlotte Brontë

ORIGINS OF MODERNISM
VOLUME 9
GARLAND REFERENCE LIBRARY OF THE HUMANITIES
VOLUME 1887

# ORIGINS OF MODERNISM

TODD K. BENDER, *Series Editor*

# Literary Impressionism in Jean Rhys, Ford Madox Ford, Joseph Conrad, and Charlotte Brontë

Todd K. Bender

Garland Publishing, Inc.
New York and London
1997

Library of Congress Cataloging-in-Publication Data

Bender, Todd K.
    Literary impressionism in Jean Rhys, Ford Madox Ford, Joseph Conrad,
and Charlotte Brontë / by Todd K. Bender.
        p.    cm. — (Garland reference library of the humanities ; vol.
1887. Origins of modernism ; vol. 9)
        Includes bibliographical references and index.
        ISBN 0-8153-1943-6 (alk. paper)
        1. English fiction—20th century—History and criticism.   2. Impres-
sionism in literature.   3. Art and literature—Great Britain—History—20th
century.   4. Modernism (Literature)—Great Britain.   5. Ford, Ford Madox,
1873–1939—Technique.   6. Conrad, Joseph, 1857–1924—Technique.
7. Rhys, Jean—Technique.   8. Positivism in literature.   9. Fiction—Technique.   10. Authorship—Collaboration.   I. Title.   II. Series: Garland reference library of the humanities ; vol. 1887.   III. Series: Garland reference
library of the humanities. Origins of modernism ; vol. 9.
    PR888.I57B46   1997
    823.009'11—dc21                                                97-10566
                                                                        CIP

Printed on acid-free, 250-year-life paper
Manufactured in the United States of America

*This book is dedicated to*

*Kirsten A. Bender*
*and*
*Claire E. Bender*

# Contents

# SERIES PREFACE

The Modernist Movement, characterized by the works of T.S. Eliot, James Joyce, Virginia Woolf, William Faulkner, and writers of similar stature, dominated Anglo-American literature for some fifty years following World War I. By the time the United States emerged from its military involvement in Indo-China in the 1970s, the Modernist Movement had disintegrated into Post-Modernism. High Modernism's most proud claim was that it would "make it new," that it represented a radical and sudden break with previous cultural traditions. We now see this claim to be false. Nowhere is Modernism more derivative than in its claim to radical novelty. The Modernist "revolution" of the twentieth century is best seen as the culmination of ideology developing in the late nineteenth century. This series of books is devoted to the study of the origins of Modernism in the half-century between the Franco-Prussian War and the First World War, from the death of Dickens to the Roaring Twenties and the Lost Generation.

As drama is the center of the literature of the Elizabethan Age, so criticism is the focus of the Modernist Age. Modernist writers worked in an environment of university and school curricula more introspective, self-conscious, and cannibalistic than ever before. How did the philosophical and pedagogical system supporting Modernism develop? What part does feminism play in the struggle for literary domination? How do changing systems of patronage and the economy of literature influence Modernism, as a vastly expanded reading public is eventually augmented by cinema, radio, and television? Do the roots of cultural pluralism within English literature trace back to the Victorian era? When English is used as the vehicle for expression of American, Canadian, Australian, or Indian culture; or for Afro-American, Hispano-American, Asian-American, or Amero-Indian culture, where do the origins of this eclectic pluralism lie?

We believe that there are two important groups of writers essential to the development of Modernism: (1) Gerard Manley Hopkins and the circle of his correspondents (Robert Bridges, Coventry Patmore, Canon Richard Watson Dixon, and related figures) and (2) the circle of writers surrounding Joseph Conrad (Ford Madox Ford, Henry James, Stephen Crane, and others). We especially encourage the further study of these two groups as foundation stones for the Modernist Movement, but there are many other sources important to its development.

Todd K. Bender
University of Wisconsin

# Acknowledgements

Bits and pieces of this book have appeared previously in *Criticism*, *Conradiana*, *Studies in the Literary Imagination*, and in programs on "literary impressionism" at annual meetings of the Modern Language Association. Work on it was begun with a fellowship from the American Council of Learned Societies and concluded during sabbatical leave generously provided by the University of Wisconsin-Madison.

# Abbreviations

Page references for quoted matter are incorporated into the text. Unless otherwise indicated, translations are my own.

Garland Publishing, Inc. has published concordances to nearly all the works of Joseph Conrad, as well as to Ford Madox Ford's *The Good Soldier* and to Charlotte Brontë's *Jane Eyre*. References to these texts are cited in this study using the concordance notation. Thus a quotation from *Lord Jim* followed by the notation (123.45-67) indicates that the passage cited falls between lines 45 and 67 of page 123 in the Field of Reference of *A Concordance to Conrad's* Lord Jim, edited by James W. Parins, Robert J. Dilligan, and Todd K. Bender (New York: Garland Publishing, Inc., 1976). A few of the concordances published by Garland list only line numbers, with no page number. For example, a quotation from Conrad's "Heart of Darkness" followed by the notation (134-42) means that the quoted matter falls between line 134 and line 142 in the Field of Reference of *A Concordance to Conrad's* "Heart of Darkness," (New York: Garland Publishing, Inc., 1979).

Abbreviations for frequently quoted texts are:

## For Conrad's works

HD = *A Concordance to Conrad's* "Heart of Darkness." Edited by Todd K. Bender. New York: Garland Publishing, Inc., 1979.

LJ = *A Concordance to Conrad's* Lord Jim. Edited by James W. Parins, Robert J. Dilligan, and Todd K. Bender. New York: Garland Publishing, Inc., 1976.

INH = *A Concordance to Conrad's* The Mirror of the Sea *and* The Inheritors. Edited by Todd K. Bender. New York: Garland Publishing, Inc., 1983.

NOS = *A Concordance to Conrad's* Nostromo. Edited by James W. Parins, Robert J. Dilligan, and Todd K. Bender. New York: Garland Publishing, Inc., 1984.

UWE = *A Concordance to Conrad's* Under Western Eyes. Edited by David Leon Higdon and Todd K. Bender. New York: Garland Publishing, Inc., 1983.

SLY = *Concordances to Conrad's* The Shadow Line and Youth: A Narrative. Edited by Todd K. Bender. New York: Garland Publishing, Inc., 1980.

**For Charlotte Brontë's works**

JE = A *Concordance to Brontë's* Jane Eyre. Edited by C. Ruth Sabol and Todd K. Bender. New York: Garland Publishing, Inc., 1981.

**For Ford Madox Ford's works**

GS = A *Concordance to Ford Madox Ford's* The Good Soldier. Edited by C. Ruth Sabol and Todd K. Bender. New York: Garland Publishing, Inc., 1981.

JC = Ford, Ford Madox. *Joseph Conrad: A Personal Remembrance*. London: Duckworth & Co., 1924.

ML = Ford, Ford Madox. *The March of Literature from Confucius to Modern Times*. London: George Allen and Unwin, Ltd., 1939.

PE = Ford, Ford Madox. *Parade's End*. New York: Vintage Books, 1979.

# INTRODUCTION
## TWO MEETINGS

*Two Key Encounters in the Modernist Revolution. Literary Impressionism. Receptive Mental Activity. Subject Versus Object. Bergsonian Vitalism. Render an Affair. Suppression of Author. Dramatic Monologue. Verbal Collage: Fragmentation, Defamiliarization, Juxtaposition, Incrementation. Constructive Reader. Open Versus Closed Texts. Pedagogy of Impressionism. The Ocular Trope.*

In the autumn of 1898, Joseph Conrad (Josef Konrad Korzeniowski, 1857-1924) met for the first time Ford Madox Ford (Ford Madox Hueffer, 1873-1939). A quarter of a century later in the summer of 1924, Jean Rhys (1894-1979) entered on her brief affair with Ford in Paris. These two intense, stormy encounters separated by a quarter of a century provide the environment in which a remarkable series of modernist masterpieces of fiction first took shape. To Ford the two meetings seemed linked together because both appear to be steps in what he called, in his *Joseph Conrad: A Personal Remembrance* (1924) and his *The March of Literature from Confucius to Modern Times* (1938), the movement of modern literature toward *impressionism*. What does Ford mean by *impressionism* and what place does Ford's idea of literary impressionism have in the modernist revolution?

Conrad and Ford were close friends and artistic collaborators from 1898 until the spring of 1904. They remained on friendly terms from 1904 until a bitter quarrel early in 1909 generated hostility between them, which gradually modulated over the remaining fifteen years of Conrad's life. In 1898, when Conrad and Ford first met, Conrad was over forty years old, having spent his boyhood with his Polish patriot father in Czarist penal settlements and his youth and young manhood sailing the remote corners of the world as an adventurous ship's officer. Conrad, whose mother tongue was Polish and whose preferred language for conversation was French, wrote all his fiction laboriously in English. The much younger Ford, who was also polyglot, and spoke French easily, seems to have helped free Conrad's English tongue so that his wealth of raw material could more easily flow into his English novels and stories.

The meeting of Conrad and Ford corresponded to a burst of creativity in Conrad's career: *Lord Jim* (1901), "Heart of Darkness" in the *Youth* volume (1902), *Typhoon* (1902), *Nostromo* (1904), as well as his acknowledged collaborations with Ford in *The Inheritors* (1901) and *Romance* (1903), which are much less accomplished works. Ford in his obituary memoir *Joseph Conrad: A Personal Remembrance* and in his *The March of Literature from Confucius to Modern Times* depicts himself playing a very important role in Conrad's creative effort. According to Ford the two writers would talk long into the night until they had a fictional scene in oral rough draft in French, then they would laboriously translate the text into written English. Although Ford's claim is perhaps extravagant, there is no doubt that, in addition to their openly collaborative texts, Ford had a hand in the composition of works like *Lord Jim*, usually attributed solely to Conrad. Ford maintains that his meeting with Conrad was momentous for Western literature because it was a step in what he calls the march of literature toward *literary impressionism*.

Ford's claim that the heightened power of Conrad's works after 1898 was the result of *literary impressionism* was made after Conrad's death in 1924 and was sharply refuted by the widow, Jessie Conrad. Between Conrad's first meeting with Ford and his death, the Great War of 1914-18 intervened, destroying the whole pattern of life in late Victorian/Edwardian England and changing the political, economic, and social fabric of Europe. When Ford advanced his claim in 1924 that literary impressionism was the key to his collaboration with Conrad, Ford was struggling to keep afloat his international literary magazine *The Transatlantic Review* and living on the Left Bank in Paris in a world very different from that of the late Victorian period when he was closely associated with Conrad. Nevertheless, when Ford met Jean Rhys in Paris in 1924, once again the encounter initiated a remarkable burst of artistic creativity for both writers. What caused the creative impulse to flourish? Is there some way in which Ford's meeting with Rhys replays his earlier encounter with Conrad?

Ford's *Transatlantic Review* ran less than two years, but in that brief span of time in 1924-25, as editor in chief, Ford gathered a remarkable stable of writers together. Of his own work, Ford serialized in *The Transatlantic Review* sections from the Tietjens novel, *Some Do Not . . .* ; from his collaboration with Conrad, parts of *The Nature of a Crime*; and short critical essays which were later partly recycled in *The March of Literature from Confucius to Modern Times*. Poems by E. E. Cummings (1894-1963), Ezra Pound (1885-1972), H. D. (Hilda Doolittle, 1886-1961), William Carlos Williams (1883-1963), Paul Valery (1871-1945); prose pieces by Gertrude Stein (1874-1946), James Joyce (1882-1941), Ernest Hemingway (1899-1961), Ring Lardner (1885-1933), and Jean Rhys (1894-1979); and letters by Joseph Conrad (1857-1924), Thomas Hardy (1840-1928), H. G. Wells (1866-1946), and T. S. Eliot (1888-1965), along with works by many other important, but lesser known, literary and artistic figures pack the pages of *The Transatlantic Review*. Ford's litmus test for authentic art fit to publish in his review was the degree by which a text tended toward what he called "literary impressionism."

In 1924 Ford was at the height of his creative power, engaged in writing his Tietjens tetralogy. While living with Stella Bowen in Paris, he met the beautiful, distressed, young, West Indian actress and author, Jean Rhys. Ford undoubtedly helped Rhys to begin her career as a writer, but when their relationship became intimate, Stella Bowen and Ford arranged for Rhys to leave Paris. After a flurry of publications in the late 1920s and early 1930s, Rhys fell silent and was forgotten as a writer until her rediscovery shortly before the publication of her masterpiece *Wide Sargasso Sea* (1966), which was greeted by *The New York Times* as evidence that she was the greatest living English novelist at that time.

Brilliant as the novel *Wide Sargasso Sea* and its filmed version are, Rhys owes much to Ford and the tradition of literary impressionism. It does not diminish her accomplishment as a writer to suggest that her work deserves to be read with impressionist masterpieces like Conrad's "Heart of Darkness" and his *Lord Jim* or Ford's *The Good Soldier* and his Tietjens tetralogy.

Does Ford's theory of *impressionism* in his memoir of Conrad or in his *March of Literature from Confucius to Modern Times* define a significant connection between Ford's encounter with Conrad in 1898 and his meeting with Rhys twenty-five years later? Does Ford's notion help to explain the artistic power of works like Conrad's *Lord Jim*, Ford's Tietjens tetralogy called *Parade's End*, and Rhys's *Wide Sargasso Sea*? Does Ford's idea of impressionism help to place his own fiction in his close collaboration with Conrad and in his relationship with Rhys?

Three strands entwine in Ford's idea of "literary impressionism": first, there is a parallel with the development of French Impressionist painting in the late Nineteenth Century; second, there is a connection between rendering impressions and taking scientific observations prior to forming generalizations, as in the "positivist" sociological methods of Auguste Comte (1798-1857) or the biological observations of Charles Darwin (1809-82); third, "impressionism" refers to British empirical philosophy, which gives priority to sensory impressions in the formation of human consciousness.

"Scientific" impressionist painting as practiced by Georges Seurat (1859-91) or Paul Cezanne (1839-1906), "positivist" sociological inquiry as advocated by Auguste Comte (1798-1857) or Emile Zola (1840-1902), and "impressionist" philosophy as developed in the followers of David Hume (1711-76) or John Locke (1632-1704) intertwine in Ford's imagination and have a powerful shaping force in his definition of the conventions of literary fiction, both in prose narrative and in poetry. Ford foregrounds the activity of perception in a receptive mind, rather than the ostensible object perceived. At first glance, we might say that his idea of literature is subjective rather than objective, but such crude polarity soon breaks down.

A "realist" imagines that there is an objective world which exists whether or not it is perceived and that the artist mirrors or reflects that exterior world in art, for example, as a photograph. An "*ex*pressionist," on the other hand, imagines that we can only know that we have mental life. The function of art is to express and make visible that inner world, for example, as instrumental music, without imitating any exterior object, expresses feelings and emotions deeply hidden in the individual mind, otherwise inaccessible to an audience. The "*im*pressionist," however, imagines that art captures the fleeting moment of intersection when the exterior world impinges on a sensitive consciousness.

The intersection of an object and subject in the senses occurs in fiction on two levels: when the story teller registers an impression of the world and when the reader registers an impression of the text. Such an instantaneous moment of consciousness reflects the idea of vitalism in the philosophy of Henri Bergson (1859-1941). That moment, and that moment alone, is living. Everything else is dead, mechanical, and inauthentic. At its core, the authentic instant, like the kernal of a nut, lies enclosed in its shell. Like Robert Browning's idea of an "infinite moment" which defines the true self under its onion skins of false seeming, the perceptive mind of the impressionist touches its stimulus and in that instant truly lives.

The literary impressionist must "render an affair," according to Ford, thinking perhaps of the French "Dreyfus Affair" or an illicit sexual "affair" as prototype. In rendering an affair, the interest lies not so much in the events which have already happened, the mere facts of the case, but in the process by which we come to see the facts in growing concentric circles of understanding, like rings surrounding a pebble thrown in a calm pool.

In Joseph Conrad's *Lord Jim*, the central scandalous affair, Jim's abandonment of the pilgrim ship, the Patna, has already happened when the story begins. The readers' interest in the work lies in the growing complexity of our understanding of the bald facts of the case. As the main narrator of the story, Marlow, says in the opening paragraph of Chapter Six of *Lord Jim*:

> There was no incertitude as to facts— . . . Yet, as I've told you, all the sailors in the port attended [Jim's trial], and the water side business was fully represented. Whether they knew it or not, the interest that drew them there was purely psychological—the expectation of some essential disclosure as to the strength, the power, the horror, of human emotions. Naturally nothing of the kind could be disclosed. The examination of the only man able and willing to face it was beating futilely round the well-known fact, and the play of questions upon it was as instructive as the tapping with a hammer on an iron box, were the object to find out what's inside. (66.05-22)

The mere fact of the affair, like an iron box, is something given, obvious, inert, well known: Jim abandoned the Patna; Kurtz decorated his hut with human heads in "Heart of Darkness"; Edward Ashburnham committed suicide in Ford Madox Ford's *The Good Soldier*; Rochester's mad West Indian wife has escaped her attic confinement and burned his house in Charlotte Brontë's *Jane Eyre* before Jean Rhys reopens the affair in *Wide Sargasso Sea*. In all these cases, the impressionist's interest shifts from the mere events of the plot to the process of ratiocination in an intelligence perceiving those events.

What Ford calls "rendering an affair" requires certain shifts in the conventions of narrative. The authorial voice must be suppressed, so that the story is told indirectly through a mask or persona, utilizing the convention of impersonation, as Browning does in his dramatic monologues like "My Last Duchess," "Bishop Blougram's Apology," "The Bishop at St. Praxed's Orders his Tomb," or the multiple monologues used to render the affair of *The Ring and the Book* (1868-69). *Lord Jim* and "Heart of Darkness" are not about the doings of Jim and Kurtz so much as they are about the growing mental awareness of Marlow, the limited, unreliable narrator who tells us about their affairs. Or, in a similar way in Ford Madox Ford's *The Good Soldier*, the story seems to focus more on the obtuse observer, Dowell, who tells us so much more than he understands, rather than on the affairs of Edward Ashburnham.

Once attention has shifted from an exterior event to the way that event makes an impression on a perceiving mind, making the protagonist of the story the observer, rather than the object observed, narrative point of view becomes a key element in the text. Eccentric, unusual, distorted by drugs, pain, or mania, the point of view through which the reader gains access to the affair takes on an augmented importance. Consider the physical disposition of reporter in the opening paragraph of Part II of "Heart of Darkness." Marlow tells us that one evening he had been sleeping on the deck of his wrecked boat on the edge of the Congo River when he heard voices approaching the bank. He identifies the speakers as the Manager of the station and his confidant. In the dusk, as Marlow drowses in and out of sleep, the pair stroll back and forth in and out of earshot with Marlow lying flat on the deck, just above their line of sight. Marlow therefore registers only fragments of their speech.

Marlow's eccentric location and imperfect ability to observe the scene resembles the handling of point of view in certain Japanese woodcuts. We see the scene literally from a very unusual angle, eccentrically supine on the boat's deck above the pair talking in the dusk, further obscured by the movement of the speakers strolling in and out of the range of our hearing and by a reporter who is drifting in and out of consciousness. Figuratively, we see the scene from an unusual angle as well, from the viewpoint of Marlow, who is a man set apart from the general or common understanding of affairs. If we define "critical realism" as questioning the reality of what is commonly considered or believed to be the case, then the eccentric observers like Conrad's Marlow and Rhys's Antoinette (the madwoman in Rochester's attic in Charlotte Brontë's *Jane Eyre*) are instruments of critical realism. They force us to reconsider, to look again, at our assumptions and judgments from an unusual, unexpected angle.

Foregrounding the point of view, constructing an eccentric, limited, "unreliable" narrator, involves reinterpreting "reality," even reordering space and time in psychological configurations, rather than as commonly experienced with three dimensional space existing in a time scheme which is linear, univocal, and one-way. As the narrator of Ford's *The Good Soldier* explains in the opening paragraph of Part Four:

> When one discusses an affair—a long, sad affair—one goes back, one goes forward. One remembers points that one has forgotten and one explains them all the more minutely since one recognizes that one has forgotten to mention them in their proper places and that one may have given, by omitting them, a false impression. I console myself with thinking that this is a real story and that, after all, real stories are probably told best in the way a person telling a story would tell them. They will then seem most real. (209.09-19)

The narrator of Ford's *The Good Soldier*, Dowell, imagines himself sitting by the fireside in a country cottage in the south of France, telling his tale by digression and interpolation, loquaciously to a friend. Perhaps Ford here imagines story telling in a pastoral or elegiac vein. Ford and Conrad were, of course, caught up in the world of modern commercial publishing. They both desperately needed to sell books to an anonymous audience. Perhaps Ford longs for a  pre-capitalist kind of story telling, when hearer and teller sit together as friends intimately joined by a communal hearth, so that the dramatized narrations of Marlow and Dowell express the longing of the real authors for an older time when the teller of tales was known personally and had a position of honor in the tribe. The activity of spinning a tale is a remedy for alienation, a cure for the estrangement of the story teller from the community.

Shifting focus in time and space to follow the mental pattern of associated ideas in the mind of the persona allows the author to exploit the power of verbal collage through fragmentation, defamiliarization, juxtaposition, and to create an "unearned increment." T. S. Eliot's "The Waste Land," like Ford Madox Ford's *The Good Soldier*, displays the gross structure of verbal collage. Linear space and time must be fragmented by taking small pieces out of context: quotations, fragments of conversation, scenes glimpsed fleetingly. These fragments, when cut away from their natural contexts, can be experienced in a "defamiliarized" way. The fragments can be seen intrinsically. So a common tool, for example, taken from its workaday context and exhibited in a museum, can be appreciated aesthetically for the graceful shape of its handle or the work-polished texture of its surface, whereas these intrinsic qualities of the thing would normally have been overlooked in its workplace where we probably see only features of the tool related to its utility.

Once fragmented and defamiliarized, fragments from widely disparate contexts can be recombined and juxtaposed into a new pattern or design in a collage. According to Ford, the whole fabric of modern art depends on this juxtaposition which creates an "unearned increment" of signification. Not only do the fragments shine with a new brightness when removed from their expected contexts and defamiliarized, they say more when taken together than they can signify separately. For example, the three tests of *Lord Jim* (Jim's failure to jump to the rescue in his training ship, his too quick jump away from the Patna, and his fatal jump to conclusions about Buccaneer Brown in Patusan) are juxtaposed in the telling of his story so that they comment on each other. Taken together the three fragmentary episodes are much more telling than when considered separately.

The "collage effect" of signification incremented through juxtaposition occurs not just in the large plot of a narrative, but also in small scale in the figurative language and metaphor of the text when tenor and vehicle are defamiliarized and brought together. In a verbal comparison or metaphor, a "vehicle" illuminates a "tenor" by signifying some point of similarity between the two and by transferring feelings elicited by the vehicle to its tenor. When T. S. Eliot begins "The Love Song of J. Alfred Prufrock" with the invitation

> Let us go then, you and I,
> When the evening is spread out against the sky
> Like a patient etherized upon a table . . .

the tenor "evening" is compared to the vehicle, a "patient etherized upon a table." The similarities shared by the two elements under comparison are such qualities as *inertness, sickliness, need of healing, waiting for a cure, helplessness,* and so on. The emotion or feelings evoked by a patient etherized, such as *fear, pity, repulsion, apprehension,* too, are transferred from vehicle to tenor. The homely evening is rendered disgusting and uncanny through its juxtaposition with an etherized patient.

At the core of impressionist texts are figurative juxtapositions both large scale and small, working by defamiliarization and juxtaposition. For example, when Marlow penetrates to the innermost station in his quest for Kurtz, he fixes his binoculars on the cottage where Kurtz dwells in the wilderness, an isolated hermitage where a follower of Jean Jacques Rousseau (1712-78) might expect to find a culturally primitive Eden regained. Marlow suddenly sees through his binoculars that Kurtz has decorated his cottage with human heads on stakes. Both in T. S. Eliot and in Conrad, the text associates two elements in the perceiving intellect: In T. S. Eliot (a) the evening is associated with (b) an etherized patient; In Conrad (a) the dwelling is associated with (b) heads on stakes. Ford in *The March of Literature from Confucius to Modern Times* and in his memoir of Joseph Conrad is keen to point out that the juxtaposition of (a) and (b) increments their meaning, making (c) a new and unexpected impression in the observing intelligence which is not found in (a) and (b) if they are taken separately.

Juxtaposition also operates in characterization where pairs or sets of characters are greatly enhanced in brilliance and signification because they are fragmentary parts of some larger whole, as simple foils, uncanny twins, shadow characters, or the doppelgaenger motif. We can imagine the contradictory impulses and hypotheses of Shakespeare's mind expressed in the constellation of all the dramatic characters in his theater. Othello and Iago are but two poles of Shakespeare's imagination. So, too, we can imagine Kurtz as a projection of the mind of Marlow, Edward Ashburnham of the mind of Dowell, and Rochester's madwoman in the attic as the expression of Jane Eyre's repressed anxieties. The public and apparent character holds the dark, hidden twin embedded in it, only to be exposed through fictional narrative. Every respectable Doctor Jekyll conceals its uncanny and altogether hideous Mr. Hyde.

Erving Goffman in *The Presentation of Self in Everyday Life* (1956) suggests that all human beings have a front or public role, as well as a back or repressed personality, and that successful dramatization of the self involves performing the front role in a tolerable manner. The inner self imagines playing a highly rewarded public role. In this way, the individual is split into a double or twinned pair. The emphasis in the narrative shifts to displaying how one plays the public role, adjusting the inner to the outer self. For example, Lord Jim as a cadet on his training ship reads schoolboy light fiction and imagines himself playing the role of hero, but his reverie is interrupted because there has been an accident at sea and the cry goes out to man the cutter for the rescue. Jim's proper place is to row stroke in the cutter, but he does not jump quickly enough to assume his role and another boy plays the hero in his place. Years later, when he is a young officer on the rusty pilgrim ship, Patna, and she is threatened with catastrophe, Jim jumps too soon into the lifeboat and so jumps away from playing the hero's role a second time. For the literary impressionist, character *is* the impression, the successful dramatization of self requiring an adjustment of the apparent front to hidden back identity.

Rooting reality in sensory impressions demands changing the plot of a novel from a report to a rendering of an affair, set in psychological time and space, thus foregrounding the process of ratiocination of the perceptive intelligence of the story teller, through indirect, limited, unreliable narration. Such innovations in the form of the novel, in turn, cast the reader in a participatory or constructive role when encountering the text.

A "closed" text will not bear repeated readings. One careful reading suffices to answer all questions raised by the story. An "open" text, on the other hand, sustains and heightens interest with each repeated reading. "Open" texts defy resolution. The big questions remain after a lifetime of savoring the work: Why does Hamlet hesitate to take his vengeance? Why does Marlow lie to the Intended Bride of Kurtz at the conclusion of "Heart of Darkness"? Is Lord Jim's death in Patusan a glorious fulfillment of his heroic quest or simply a foolish suicide? Is Jane Eyre likely to live happily ever after with Rochester, now that his madwoman in the attic is burned away?

An important dimension of impressionist literature is the "opening" of the canon. Readers of Charlotte Brontë's *Jane Eyre* thought they had closed the book and understood it well, until Rhys gave them *Wide Sargasso Sea*. Readers of Thomas Hughes's (1822-96) *Tom Brown's Schooldays* (1856) thought they had solved the mystique of the British officer class, until *Lord Jim* reopened the question. The impressionist text typically stands in a critical relation to earlier texts, forcing us to rethink afresh our judgments. It follows that Ford's literary criticism in *The March of Literature from Confucius to Modern Times* is a revaluation, a systematic reopening of the whole canon of Western literature. The general critical bent of the modernist period may be mainly an expression of the impressionist's drive to read in a constructive way, to make the reader participate in forming an impression of the text which is always open to amendment, never finally set.

One of the most important features of Ford's literary impressionism is its pedagogical impact, its potential utility for teachers and students. At American universities today, the text which is most often examined in the classroom is Conrad's "Heart of Darkness." More often than Shakespeare's *Hamlet*, much more often than Milton's *Paradise Lost* or any of the tales of Chaucer's pilgrims, students examine "Heart of Darkness" in an educational setting. Why this pedagogical focus? Cynically, we might perhaps suggest that it is conveniently short, its vocabulary elementary, its sentence structure simple. Perhaps its story is topical, tracing the impact of European imperialism on the Third World. On the other hand, it involves an almost completely male cast of characters, so that it seems out of touch with pressing concerns of many teachers and students who are interested in the role of women in society and literature. Moreover, it has recently been argued that the text is thoroughly racist, that it adopts the vocabulary and attitudes of the European exploiters of Africa. Nevertheless, this politically incorrect story holds a central place in a field of study in which more than half the students are female and many are proudly from non-European backgrounds. What is its attraction? Why should it be exempt from the disdain sometimes shown for other stories about guns and arrows, or whales, bears, and elephants?

Is it possible that the main attraction of "Heart of Darkness" for teacher and student is the framing situation of the tale. On the deck of the cruising yawl, the Nellie, the audience, composed of the director of companies, the lawyer, the accountant, and the "I" speaker, is forced to pass a period of time listening to the storyteller Marlow's exposition of what he once saw in the Congo. This company compelled to interact in response to Marlow's tale is very similar to the usual discussion section in a university classroom. Its members expose their abrasively differing interpretations of the events described. "Heart of

Darkness" is convenient for the teacher and students because it sets up a ready-made dramatized situation and invites the class to draw up a chair and join the discussion.

All the teacher and students need do is to step imaginatively into the space on the deck of the Nellie, to expand the circle of listeners there, and to react to the situations sketched by Marlow. Marlow often seems like a comic caricature of the bumbling teaching assistant addressing a circle of privileged, sheltered children in the university classroom, who are for the most part descendants of lawyers, accountants, and directors of companies. As Marlow explains his story, he appears perhaps a bit obtuse and limited at times, but nevertheless more experienced than his audience. The success of "Heart of Darkness" in the classroom is that it *represents* a classroom. It invites a variety of interpretations, a clash of opinions, a web of incompatible impressions, and prevents the reader finally from closing debate on the meaning of the bare facts reported by Marlow.

Our modern academic apparatus for the study of literature, with its discussion sections, analytic papers and examinations, close readings of texts, competing theoretical frames constantly defamiliarizing the works at hand, is perhaps the result of the march of literature toward impressionism, valuing each reader's constructive encounter with the text and treating all texts as open to multiple "interpretations." What every student today expects to "do" with a text when it is assigned as required reading for English Literature in the classroom is a recent and rather peculiar development. Only within the last century do schools systematically cultivate pedagogical strategies which value diversity of responses among students. Ford's theory of literary impressionism reinforces such institutional foregrounding of each individual reader's democratic interpretive activity. Likewise, the juxtaposition of one text with another in the usual university syllabus aims to highlight an incremented significance, revealed in the mind of each student, so as to exploit the collage effect.

The serialization of artifacts which occurs in sequences of impressionist paintings of the "same" object, like Claude Monet's (1840-1926) series of haystacks, his various renderings of the facade of Rouen Cathedral, or his many canvases of water lilies, establishes that his works of art capture only an ephemeral and fleeting impression of an object, changing under varieties of lighting and weather conditions. But the serialization of the artifacts also produces the collage effect of defamiliarization and incrementation through juxtaposition. The arrangement of Frank Lloyd Wright's (1859-1969) Guggenheim Museum in New York in its spiral sequence of modern artifacts on display is an extension of the juxtaposition of so-called "impressionist" paintings in the 1874 Exposition of the Association of Independent Artists in Paris. Probably one of the most important innovations of impressionist painting in the Nineteenth Century is in the manner of organizing and displaying art, so that the very idea of "French impressionist painting" is something constructed by viewers, who create a relationship among otherwise unconnected artifacts because they find them associated in a particular sequence in the context of the display.

Considered in juxtaposed sets or particular groups, individual paintings become much more meaningful than when they stand isolated separately. Ford exploits a similar serialization of art in his *March of Literature from Confucius to Modern Times*. He creates a collage of literary history in which his own work, as well as that of Conrad and Rhys, sparkles with an unusual brilliance, defamiliarized and juxtaposed alongside carefully chosen texts by Gustave Flaubert (1821-1880), Guy de Maupassant (1850-93), Henry James (1843-1916), or Stephen Crane (1871-1900). Serialization of the sort found in *March of Literature from Confucius to Modern Times* is one of the most common practices in the study of literature in modern schools and universities. Not only does the serialization emphasize the process by which each reader must form connections among individual texts, but also serialization creates an avant-garde and opens the canon. The series always aches for its final step, its missing conclusion. The serialization creates a sense of direction and a teleology in what would otherwise be a chaotic jumble of unrelated texts.

By mounting the psychological reaction of the unreliable, limited narrator onto the bald spectacle of the affair and by forcing the reader into a participatory role in encountering the text, the impressionist writer alters and extends the possibilities of literary form. Ezra Pound had published two of his *Cantos* in volume 1, number 1, of Ford Madox Ford's *The Transatlantic Review*, and Pound's idea of constant formal renewal, "making it new," pervades the criticism of Ford and the general artistic project of literary impressionism.

How does it happen that very few readers notice that Conrad, Ford, and Rhys are funny writers? Often the hilarious is deeply serious. The joke works like a dream to concentrate or disguise something too powerful to be spelled out consciously. The shared impression of laughter declares a community of values, sometimes between characters and dramatic audiences, at other times perhaps between narrator and reader at the expense of a character. When do impressionist texts explicitly state that a joke occurs? Who laughs and who does not join the laughter? For example, in Conrad's "Heart of Darkness," does the reader join the severed head on a pole outside Kurtz's hut "smiling continuously at some endless and jocose dream" (130)? In *Lord Jim* does the reader agree that some infernal powers had selected Jim "for the victim of their practical joke" (131.12), when he leaps from the Patna to save himself but the boat does not sink? When Jane Eyre hears uncanny laughter in the hidden chambers of Rochester's house, on whom is the joke? Impressionism provides a dark laughter reminiscent of Henry Fielding's (1707-1754) theory of the corrective power of ridicule, but the idea of laughter in Conrad, Ford, and Rhys seems more intimately connected to the vitalism of Henri Bergson.

Two of the most important ideas connected with impressionist art are the "authentic" and the "vital" quality. "Authentic" etymologically refers to the "self" (in Greek *autos*) of the artist and of the audience. In an authentic experience of art, selfhood is engaged. There is an indwelling presence or participation of the self in the act of creation and in the act of perception of the artifact. The impressionist audience cannot stand passive. For the artifact to exist at all, the audience must participate in its creation. The colors of a pointillist canvas by Seurat, for example, exist only on the retina of each viewer's eye. The optical mixture of color is actively created in each sensitive perception.

At the core of philosophic impressionism in Locke, in positivist observation in Comte, in scientific impressionist painting in Seurat, and in literary impressionism in Ford, Conrad, and Rhys lies the problem of the ocular trope. In what way is reading a text like seeing an object? What actually takes place when the mind forms an impression of something outside itself? How can such a process be captured in language? Both in the large-scale structures of persona and point of view and in the small-scale choices of individual words in the lexicon of Conrad, Ford, and Rhys there is a widespread anxiety about how impressions are formed. The authors reply to that anxiety by developing a set of technical devices for the telling of the story, such as limited narration, verbal collage, subversive laughter, open plot and characterization, and cognitive dissonance and turbulence in their texts. These are the very devices that render Conrad, Ford, and Rhys eloquent, that free their individual voices. Ford's gift to Rhys was to bring to her the impressionist concern for formal innovation. It was Rhys's gift to Conrad and Ford to carry their work forward in her powerful and original way.

# CHAPTER I
## FINEST FRENCH NOVEL IN ENGLISH

*The Impressionist Affair. Character split between Public Role and Private Personality. "Tension" and Empathy. Joseph Conrad, Ford Madox Ford, and the French Background of Literary Impressionism in Emile Zola (1840-1902), Gustave Flaubert (1821-80), and Guy de Maupassant (1850-93). Fedor Mikhailovich Dostoyevsky's (1821-81) Underground Man.*

Joseph Conrad died on August 3, 1924. Within two months, his former collaborator Ford Madox Ford rushed into print his memoir, *Joseph Conrad: A Personal Remembrance.* In the "Preface" dated October 5, 1924, Ford excuses his haste, promising that his account "contains no documentation at all; for it no dates have been looked up, even all the quotations but two have been left unverified, coming from the author's memory. It is the writer's *impression* of a writer who avowed himself *impressionist.* Where the writer's memory has proved to be at fault over a detail afterwards out of curiosity looked up, the writer has allowed the fault to remain on the page; but as to the truth of the *impression* as a whole the writer believes that no man would care—or dare—to impugn it" (JC 6). As was often the case in Ford's career, his expectations proved overly optimistic.

After an initially rather favorable public reception of Ford's tribute, on December 4, 1924, Conrad's widow, Jessie, registered an enraged protest at the blatant untruth of the "detestable book" in the *Times Literary Supplement.* Her hostility to Ford was of long standing. She had never liked Ford's loose ways with women and money and she may have been somewhat jealous of the time her husband spent working with him. The friendship between Conrad and Ford had cooled in the last fifteen years of Conrad's life so that they had not been closely associated for many years when Ford wrote his memoir. Apparently the grief-stricken widow, Jessie, now saw Ford's book as a cheap attempt by a hack writer to exploit her husband's reputation. By fabricating claims to have participated in the creation of Conrad's novels, Ford seemed to reduce Conrad to a quasi-comic foreigner guided through the mysteries of the English language and literature by his young collaborator.

Jessie Conrad's anger is understandable and her attack no doubt contributed to the generally unsavoury atmosphere surrounding Ford's character in the years between the two World Wars. Her hostility also contributed to the eclipse of Ford's reputation as a writer following his death in 1939 until the revival of his masterpiece, *The Good Soldier,* in the late 1950's. While Ford is today usually considered to be one of the keystones of the modernist movement in literature, ranked along with writers like T. S. Eliot and James Joyce, such a favorable evaluation is relatively new, not generally prevalent before about 1970. When Ford fell into oblivion after his death, his idea of "literary impressionism" was also obscured, along with his claim that Conrad was an avowed "impressionist." The idea of literary impressionism, however, may help readers to understand the contribution of Ford and Conrad to the modernist movement and to see the lineage of three generations of modernist writers in Conrad, Ford, and Jean Rhys.

The autumn of 1924 was a difficult time for Ford. The death of Conrad was not only followed by Jessie's devastating attack on his memoir, but Ford's journal *The Transatlantic Review* was careening toward financial collapse. His personal affairs were in even more disarray than usual, as he was living with Stella Bowen, while involved with the young West Indian woman, Jean Rhys, who since the 1960s also claims for herself a place as one of the most important modernist writers. In addition to her best known and most effective novel, *Wide Sargasso Sea* (1966), her works include *Quartet* (so titled in 1929, originally published as *Postures*), *Voyage in the Dark* (1934), *Good Morning, Midnight* (1939), and the bitter *After Leaving Mr. Mackenzie* (1930), which exposes her 1924 affair, with Ford transparently portrayed as the despicable male central character.

The year 1924 was also a period of intense artistic creativity for Ford, in the midst of writing his Tietjens Tetralogy usually called *Parade's End* composed of *Some Do Not . . .* (1924), *No More Parades* (1925), *A Man Could Stand Up* (1926), and *Last Post* (1928). In August and September of 1924, while Ford hastily wrote up his recollections of his association with Conrad nearly thirty years before, he was precariously balanced. Would the Tietjens Tetralogy combine with *The Good Soldier,* as well as his many other published works, to assure him a place in the history of European letters? Or would his financial, sexual, and literary extravagances disgrace him and eradicate his claim to fame and honor once and for all?

Jessie Conrad is correct to describe Ford's *Joseph Conrad: A Personal Remembrance* as shocking. It is outrageous both for what it *is* and for what it *says.* We expect it to about Conrad, but the author manages to put the emphasis on himself, the seeing eye registering his impressions of Conrad. We expect the book to be based to a great degree on fact, but it is clearly fiction—-perhaps more remote from real historical events than Conrad's own fictions like "Heart of Darkness" or *Almayer's Folly.* In his "Preface," Ford maintains that this memoir is "written by an artist and . . . [is] a work of art." He warns his readers that it "is a novel, not a monograph; a portrait, not a narration: for what it shall prove to be worth, a work of art, not a compilation" (JC 6). In effect, *Joseph Conrad: A Personal Remembrance* is a strange kind of new novel, not a historical record.

*Joseph Conrad: A Personal Remembrance* must be seen as historical fiction in the manner of Ford's earlier Fifth Queen trilogy, including *The Fifth Queen: And*

*How She Came to Court* (1906), *Privy Seal: His Last Venture* (1907), and *Fifth Queen Crowned: A Romance* (1908). In novels like the *Fifth Queen Crowned: A Romance,* Ford had taken the undoubtedly real character of King Henry VIII and constructed for him imaginary scenes, fictional conversations, and invented motives and states of mind. Why, after all, should he not do the same for his former friend, Joseph Conrad. To Jessie Conrad and others close to her late husband, the fictionalization of Conrad seemed an insult to his memory, an exercise in bad taste. Yet, unless we want to shut ourselves off from whatever value Ford's memoir may contain, we must accept it for what it is: a bold experiment in the relation of fiction to reality, something on the order of Robert Coover's *The Public Burning* or John Dos Passos's *U.S.A.*, a forerunner of the New Journalist's fiction, boldly mingling historical fact with fiction and fantasy in an incongruous collage.

Although Ford's *Joseph Conrad: A Personal Remembrance* is ostensibly talking about his collaboration with Conrad in the late 1890's and their joint creation of works such as *Romance*, "Heart of Darkness," and *Lord Jim,* no reader can believe for a minute that Ford is giving an "accurate" description of the historical situation when he and Conrad worked together. Ford takes the invention of Lord Jim and Charlie Marlow in the 1890s as a vehicle to make a statement about the feelings he has for his own creative act in 1924. As he imagines it, his collaboration with Conrad incarnates a vast spirit of the age, a new direction in art exhibited only imperfectly in fragmentary moments: in Conrad's Marlow, in Ford's Dowell, and in a series of works by Gustave Flaubert, Henry James, Virginia Woolf, James Joyce, Stephen Crane, and related writers, who demonstrate the evolution of "literary impressionism" as a turning point in the movement toward high modernism.

No matter that these works are scattered over a long span of time and are in some cases historically unconnected one to another. In the memoir of Conrad and in Ford's later *The March of Literature from Confucius to Modern Times,* bits and pieces of reality twist in Ford's mind into a new and fanciful configuration, the rise of literary impressionism. His collaboration with Conrad takes on a peculiar significance in this movement. Conrad becomes transformed from a flesh and blood person into a fictional character, an unwitting token caught in a web of historical forces. He becomes part of a series. His works are displayed in a constellation, a intellectual framework, or arrangement, like the series of canvases on the walls of the *Exposition* in 1874 at the first so-called "impressionist" exhibition in Paris. The most powerful innovation in the 1874 *Exposition* is perhaps in its method of display, bringing works of art into association only because the independent artists who produce them share aesthetic objectives. The *Exposition,* like Ford's exposition of *The March of Literature from Confucius to Modern Times,* created a collage of artifacts brought into a pattern because of shared technique, despite widely differing subject matter.

The protagonist of Ford's historical novel *Joseph Conrad: A Personal Remembrance* is not a man, but a stereotypical icon, an image making visible what Ford imagined to be a historically inevitable sweep, the literate world's march toward impressionism. Conrad in *Joseph Conrad: A Personal Remembrance* is like Ford's earlier portrait of King Henry VIII in the Fifth Queen Trilogy, who is imagined to be caught in the inevitable historical tide sweeping England out of the Roman Catholic organization, even though he is reluctant and only vaguely understands his role in that great movement. Conrad, like King Henry VIII, is an obtuse observer of a major shift in Western culture. The obtuse observer is often funny, blinking in calm puzzlement as the world falls apart around him, like Captain McWhirr in the eye of the hurricane in Conrad's "Typhoon."

In *The March of Literature from Confucius to Modern Times,* Ford's controlling idea is that ancient Chinese literature established a polarity, which has dominated all the subsequent literature in the world, an opposition between the way of Confucius and the way of Lao-Tsze: "We may say that Confucius tried by his teachings, his writings and his anthologies to induce men, for the purposes of better government of human affairs, to become 'superior'—as who should say 'gentlemen'" (ML 40). The followers of Confucius studied to become literati, mandarins, to take part in the administration of vast governmental departments, to attain positions in a hierarchy. Lao-Tsze, on the other hand, was an "individualist-quietist" (ML 41), who withdrew from the futile ambitions and pursuits of the mandarin into the self-sufficient life of a pastoral hermit.

The pattern of antagonistic alternatives in Confucius versus Lao-Tsze seems to Ford to repeat itself over and over in the sweep of history, for example in the opposition of the mandarin Voltaire (1694-1778) versus the pastoral Jean Jacques Rousseau (1712-1778) in France. However fanciful this alleged opposition between the active man versus the eremite may be as a description of ancient Chinese thought, it certainly is a succinct statement of a major ideological tension in Ford's fiction in general. For example, in the Tietjens Tetralogy, does not Christopher Tietjens hesitate between the life of a Confucian mandarin versus that of pastoral withdrawal? So, too, in Conrad's fiction the reader often finds the active man confronted by his passive mirror, Kurtz or Lord Jim seen by Marlow. Perhaps it would be more accurate to find the opposition of active hero versus passive observer residing in two aspects of certain single characters, such as the withdrawn story teller Marlow on the deck of the Nellie passively considering his previous more active life in the Congo. In this way the text combines in Marlow's identity two roles: the more youthful swashbuckling river-boat captain now emerging from the memory of the quiet story teller, replaying Lao-Tsze's imagined confrontation with Confucius, as the elder Marlow confronts his former more youthful self.

In *The March of Literature from Confucius to Modern Times,* Ford restates a common topic in Conrad's fiction: there is a tension between the active and the passive, the agent and the observer, like that between the agent Kurtz and the observer Marlow, or between Ford's active Edward Ashburnham versus the passive Dowell. As Erving Goffman in *The Presentation of Self in Everyday Life* points out, the internalization of this opposition in such phrases as "I see myself" splits a single character into two identities, the *homo duplex* who combines in a single character both agent and observer. So in the opening pages of Conrad's Lord Jim, Jim is described as a boy given to reading light literature of life at sea. As he reads, Jim *"saw himself* saving people from sinking ships, cutting away masts in a hurricane, swimming through surf with a line; or as a lonely castaway, barefooted and half naked, walking on uncovered reefs in search of shell-fish to stave off starvation" (emphasis provided, LJ 5.09-14).

Jim "saw himself." Jim must be considered as a split personality, *homo duplex*, one part of his character observing the other. The whole of the novel concerns how difficult it is for Jim, the agent, to play the public role of schoolboy hero which is so forcefully defined by light fiction in the eyes of the observing, self-conscious, judging part of his character. From this split between the public role versus the private personality, the action of the entire novel develops, as Jim strives to live up to the image he has of himself as a public hero.

Throughout the private lives of Conrad and Ford there is a remarkable effort at impersonation and role-playing. The very names "Joseph Conrad" and "Ford Madox Ford" are, of course, pseudonyms assumed in order to play a foreign role more easily. Each biography displays a painful process of becoming, striving to match the approved and rewarded expectations of others. We can imagine Conrad, as a boy, leaping away from his inherited identity as the son of a political prisoner or martyred Polish patriot to become first a naval officer, then a man of English letters, each stage of his development requiring a painful negation of his previous identity, a betrayal of some treasured values in his family, homeland, and native tongue.

Ford, too, traveled under a  false name, a first generation immigrant to England, always pretending to be someone he was not, always wracked by guilt for playing his role imperfectly, whether as Pre-Raphaelite boy genius, faithful husband and fatherly patron, the intellectual focus of Western culture between the wars, or merely an aging mid-Western college professor. He was always haunted by a sense of failure and the guilty denial of his innermost self. For both Conrad and Ford the vital or authentic link between private personality and public role was fragile.

In Ford's *Joseph Conrad: A Personal Remembrance*, the private individual, Conrad, comes in conflict with the social role dictated for him by his historical circumstances. He is struggling to become a commercial success as a writer. Such an ambition discourages telling unpopular truths. The reading public often rewards telling popular lies. Moreover, writers seldom become rich because of their aesthetically pure style. When Ford creates his fictional character "Joseph Conrad," he delineates the conflict in Conrad between what his inner voice demands and what a writer must do to win external success and rewards. As a riverboat officer in training, Conrad personally witnessed at first hand the atrocious conditions in the Congo. Like Marlow, Conrad hesitated to publish what he had seen. Public opinion acts as a censor both for Conrad and for his fictive persona, Marlow.

Ford's character "Joseph Conrad" must be considered set apart from the flesh and blood, retired sea captain originally from Poland, once baptized as Jozef Teodor Konrad Korzeniowski. To emphasize the difference between Ford's literary creation and the living man who called himself Joseph Conrad, we might refer to Ford's fictionalized character as "Joseph," or simply by the letter "J" for Joseph or "K" for Konrad, rather like Kafka referring indirectly to himself as "K."

"J" or "K," Ford's literary invention, demonstrates a family resemblance to many of Conrad's own fictional characters. For example, "J" is forced into a public role. He has to say and do what is pleasing to his audience, only indirectly indicting the cruelties he recorded in his Congo diary and delaying publication of the material in "Heart of Darkness" until years after his actual experiences, lest he offend the missionary and imperial attitudes of his readers. He is like Lord J-im falling into line with the social role demanded of a good naval officer, no matter how painful and personally destructive it may be for him. Similarly, he is like K-urtz caught up in the system of European exploitation of Africa, playing his commercial role finally to the hilt. Ford argues in his memoir that while Conrad was writing *about* the fate of a simple British seaman like Lord Jim who gradually becomes the public role provided to him by his place and time, "J" himself was painfully forced into a role.

*Literary Impressionism* for Ford was characterized by a set of technical features which are recognized today, but which were seldom explicitly defined at the turn of this century. In general, impressionist fiction "suppresses" the author from the pages of the book by utilizing a limited, dramatized *persona* as story teller, the screen or recipient for impressions, the camera eye. Impressionism in the novel develops from the poetic dramatic monologue as practiced, for example, by Robert Browning. An invented persona speaks to an invented audience in a dramatized situation, as the Duke in Browning's "My Last Duchess" speaks to the emissary arranging his future wedding contract while they gaze at the portrait of the Duke's former wife, now dead.

Conrad's Marlow or Ford's Dowell, in a manner similar to Browning's Duke, stand between the real author and the real reader. The persona tells the tale to a dramatic audience clearly different from the real reader. The story is told in a dramatized setting with at least four "levels": real author (like Conrad), story telling persona (like Marlow), dramatic audience (the director of companies, lawyer, accountant, and "I" on the deck of the Nellie in "Heart of Darkness"), and real audience (the reader whose eyes actually encounter the text).

Marlow, the storyteller in Conrad's "Heart of Darkness," or Dowell, the narrator of Ford's *The Good Soldier*, provide dramatized centers of consciousness superimposed on the spectacle of the affair so that the text proceeds indirectly, following the developing awareness of the story teller or of his dramatic audience. The text of the novel is realistic in the sense that it follows the real, or at least plausible, mental process of growing understanding in the persona and in the dramatic audience *about* a complicated affair which lies elsewhere in space and time. "Heart of Darkness" is not merely about events which have already happened in the Congo, but the text also renders how Marlow and his listeners on the deck of the Nellie, in the fictive present time, understand that history from the remote Congo.

When the past affair becomes the topic of ratiocination and discussion by the persona and his audience in present fictional time, the sequence of events loses its linear or causal organization and becomes a tangle of remembered events as the minds recall, amplify, and emend them. As Ford asserts,

> What was the matter with the novel, and the British novel in particular, was that it went straight forward, whereas in your gradual making acquaintanceship with your fellows you never do go straight forward. You meet an English gentleman at your golf club. He is beefy, full of health, the moral of the finest type. You discover gradually, that he is hopelessly neurasthenic, dishonest in matters of small change, but unexpectedly self-sacrificing, a dreadful liar but a most painfully careful student of lepidoptera and, finally, from the public prints, a bigamist who was once, under another name, hammered on the Stock Exchange . . . Still, there he is, the beefy full-fed fellow, moral of an English Public School product. To get such a man in fiction you could not begin at his beginning and work his life chronologically to the end. You must first get him in with a strong impression, and then work backwards and forwards over his past . . . That theory at least we [Conrad and Ford] gradually evolved . (JC 129-30)

The reader recognizes here the formula for Conrad's presentation of Lord Jim on the opening page of the novel, beginning with a paragraph giving a strong external description of his type, then weaving back and forth in time, building the web of incompatible contradictions underlying his impressive appearance.

Ford imagines fiction based, not on events or facts, but on perceptions of character. We perceive people in stereotypical roles such as Christopher Tietjens or Edward Ashburnham as the "English Tory gentleman." Roles of this kind, however, on inspection reveal unsuspected contradiction, tension, and a fierce struggle of the private individual to fit into the public role while "really" being someone else, residing somewhere else in another dimension. If character is so conceived, then certain methods of handling narrative timing, episodes, and point of view follow.

Ford claimed that he and Conrad developed the notion that the novel must be a rendering of impressions, not a narration, and that the subject matter for the novel should be an *affair,* a network of human relationships shifting under the stress of an unusual pressure. Perhaps he was thinking of a sexual "affair" or perhaps of the Dreyfus affair in France. General Campion in *Some Do Not . . .* scolds Christopher Tietjens because he will not fit easily into the public role of a perfectly adjusted military officer, calling him "a regular Dreyfus." Christopher replies, "Did you think Dreyfus was guilty?" (PE 75). An "affair" is the unacknowledged, potential scandal when a mask of superficial respectability gives a stable, decent appearance to what is, in fact, a disgraceful situation. When the mask crumbles, it reveals beneath the respectable, calm surface of things the hidden, desperate inner turmoil of the players. For example, a sexual affair requires that at least one of the lovers have commitments elsewhere rendering the love illicit. Revelation of the affair occurs when the illicit love can no longer be masked.

With reference to the impressionist idea of an "affair," a distinction must be made between denominated concepts and undenominated concepts. A novel may be concerned with concepts which are never explicitly named, such as "guilt" or "felicity." The words "guilt" or "felicity" may never actually occur in the text, yet a careful reader can see that these undenominated concepts are key to understanding its general import. On the other hand, sometimes a text utilizes or states explicitly and repeatedly its key terms. For example, a concordance will tell the reader that the relatively short text of Conrad's "Heart of Darkness" explicitly uses the word "black" forty-three times and the word "white" thirty-seven times. Such frequent denomination of opposites suggests some thematic or ideological resonance lying behind these words.

The *Concordance to Ford Madox Ford's The Good Soldier,* shows that the words *affair* and *affairs* occur in the text forty-three times, which relatively high frequency probably indicates that the words designate a conscious or subconscious thematic concern. The concordance traces the range of signification indicated by the contexts in which the word occurs. Ford uses the words to signify three meanings: First, and by far the most frequent, *affair* refers to an illicit sexual adventure as "a love affair, a love for any definite woman—is something in the nature of a widening experience" (130.26) and so he refers to the "affair" with Dolciquita (197.25) and Maisie Maidan (210.06), as well as numerous other liaisons. A second meaning of the word is simply *business* or *state of things,* but this bland meaning frequently becomes freighted with sexual innuendo, as when Nancy Rufford innocently reads the sordid details of the Brand divorce case and finds it to be "a queer affair" (247.15). The signification of *affair* for Nancy is more limited than it is for the readers of the novel. Finally, the word *affair* is used in a technical sense to designate a particular kind of story, as Dowell describes his own process of telling this tale, "When one discusses an affair—a long, sad affair—one goes back, one goes forward. One remembers points that one has forgotten and one explains them all the more minutely since one recognizes that one has forgotten to mention them in their proper places . . ." (209.10).

The common denominator in these uses of the word is that a character in almost every case appears in a dual situation. He or she finds that society offers a public role to play, such as "the good soldier," "our man Nostromo," or "the faithful wife," but these common roles are not easily fulfilled, either because two possible roles conflict or because the private personality of the individual does not conform easily to its public role. An "affair" occurs when a character struggles to play a public role incompatible with its innermost being.

The reader is interested in the problem of adjusting private personality to public role. A story reveals the conflict and tension between those two identities most evidently in the sexual affair, where the private sexual attraction becomes illicit because it violates the role defined by society for the sexual contract of respectable wife, husband, or lover. The struggle to fulfill a role is also frequently evident in sports, as the reference to Edward Ashburnham playing polo in "a scratch affair" brilliantly stealing the ball from the German captain (32.21).

The "tension" spectators feel watching gymnastics competition or competitive games like basketball or polo appears to be empathy for the struggle or "tension" of the protagonist to fulfill an ideal role, a perfect performance dictated by judges or the rules of the game, while threatened by a fear of falling short or failing to fulfill the expected role in public. The spectators feel the tension or effort required of the player without themselves being subject to real risk or danger, so the spectators participate at a distance aesthetically from the real experience. When spectators at a gymnastics competition strain as they watch the athlete execute gravity-defying gyrations, the audience experiences "empathy," a "feeling in" the character, sharing vicariously the athlete's effort. Empathy converts the actual muscular tension of the athlete into an aesthetic experience of tension for the spectator. Similarly the readers of a novel experience empathetically the "tension" of a character struggling to fulfill incompatible or contradictory roles.

All humankind play roles defined for them by society. When it is possible to play such roles easily and to perfection, all goes smoothly and there is no need for fiction, but when the private volition of a character causes him or her pain in playing the available public role or when two public roles make conflicting demands on the player, fiction becomes a way to play out the conflict harmlessly. The core of the impressionist affair is a conflict or abrasion in playing socially acceptable roles. The technical problem for the impressionist storyteller is how to make the reader feel that tension empathetically, rather than merely naming it and talking *about* it.

Ford's masterpiece, *The Good Soldier*, concerns two married couples: Dowell (the narrator), with his wife Florence (Hurlbird) Dowell, and Edward Ashburnham, with his wife Leonora (Powys) Ashburnham. The names of the leading characters have onomastic overtones. A "dowel rod" in cabinet work or carpentry fastens together a joint. The narrator Dowell holds together the intersection of the two families, the two continents, the two sexes in Ford's text. Or, perhaps, "Dowell" should be pronounced "do well," when it is possible to "do better" or even "do best." Dowell does well, or satisfies the lowest degree of righteousness, because he does not actively commit sin; but fails to take positive action to promote virtue, which might be described as doing better or doing the best. Or, perhaps, "Dowell" is to be pronounced like "dual" or "duel." Dowell and Ashburnham are a "dual" pair, active and passive, who "duel" for survival in the modern world.

The Dowells are wealthy, leisured Americans, on extended vacation in Europe. British Captain Ashburnham is from an old landed Anglican family. His wife is an impoverished Irish Catholic. The events of the story take place between August, 1904, and August, 1913, a nine-year period throughout most of which the two couples are the best of friends, living at European spas, in elegant, cultivated, beautiful, respectable idleness. There is an elegiac tone to this work, reflecting the autumnal sunshine of the Edwardian summer, soon to be brutally wiped out by World War I. Many of the events of the story occur on August 4, the very date of the beginning of the Great War, so that the repetition of the August 4   date tolls through the text year by year foreshadowing the coming cataclysm.

The fragility of the Ashburnhams' and the Dowells' felicity is displayed in the metaphor of the minuet:

> Our intimacy was like a minuet, simply because on every possible occasion and in every possible circumstance we knew where to go, where to sit, which table we should unanimously choose . . . it can't be gone. You can't kill a minuet de la cour. You may shut up the music-book, close the harpsichord; in the cupboard and presses the rats may destroy the white satin favors. The mob may sack Versailles; the Trianon may fall, but surely the minuet—the minuet itself is dancing itself away into the furthest stars. (6.14-27)

World War I, like the French Revolution, swept away the structure and form of a privileged class. The superficially sunny and cheerful life of the Dowells and Ashburnhams in the decade before World War I was rotten at its heart and vulnerable to change.

*The Good Soldier* presents a contrast between appearance and reality. For most of the nine-year period of the action, Dowell believes that the foursome are living an ideal, decent, completely respectable idyll. True, he thinks that Florence is suffering from a heart ailment which prevents any sexual contact between himself and his wife, restricts her travel, and requires her to be shut in her room alone from time to time. In the course of the novel, Dowell learns that this tranquil appearance of peace and harmony is not true.

Dowell eventually learns, in fact, that his wife's heart is physically sound and that she has deceived him about her health so as to commit adultery, first with a despicable young man named Jimmy and later with Edward Ashburnham himself. Throughout nine years Dowell imagines that Ashburnham is a model husband, his best friend, only to learn that he has engaged in a series of affairs and that his wife Leonora does not speak to him except when required to do so in public. Finally, Dowell sees that his own wife Florence has been Ashburnham's mistress. The novel is like a hall of mirrors, as the obtuse narrator Dowell seldom knows the true state of the affairs while he sees and reports a tangle of illusions and delusions to the reader.

It is easier to hold the plot of *The Good Soldier* in mind if we rearrange it from the scrambled order in which it is told to a more customary linear sequence of events. Ashburnham, like Christopher Tietjens in Ford's tetralogy *Parade's End,* is a Tory gentleman from an old Anglican aristocratic family. The Ashburnham estate is called Branshaw Teleragh. As the novel opens he has just returned from his tour of duty as an army officer in India. He, along with his wife and her companion, young Mrs. Maidan, stop at Bad Nauheim in Germany on their return trip. In the spa hotel in Bad Nauheim the Dowells and the Ashburnhams meet for the first time. Although Ashburnham appears to be brave, sentimental, and heroic, like the perfect knights of ancient romances, the reader gradually discovers that he has been involved in a series of unfortunate affairs with women.

Ashburnham's parents arranged his marriage to Leonora Powys, a Catholic convent-educated girl, whose impoverished father is an old comrade-in-arms with Ashburnham's father and who scarcely makes a living from his estate in Ireland. Religious, financial, and temperamental differences soon cause the marriage between Ashburnham and Leonora to cool. While riding in a third class train carriage in order to save money so as to please his young wife, Ashburnham clumsily tries to comfort a crying servant girl. She misunderstands his advances and Ashburnham is arrested for sexual misbehavior in what is called the Kilsyte case. This misadventure leads him for the first time in his life to consider himself capable of bad conduct.

Ashburnham's next affair involves his short-lived passion for a Spanish dancer, La Dolciquita, who demands cash for spending a week with him at

Antibes. Reckless gambling at the casino, combined with direct expenses of La Dolciquita's passion, substantially deplete Ashburnham's inherited fortune. His wife, Leonora, makes herself the guardian of his estate and sets out to recover their financial losses. She demands that he take a military post in India for eight years and doles out his spending money carefully, while squeezing his tenants and lands back in England for as much profit as possible. She is puzzled that Ashburnham does not appreciate what she does for him.

In India, Ashburnham takes as his next mistress Mrs. Basil. Mrs. Basil's husband, who is Ashburnham's brother officer, allows the affair to go on so that he can blackmail Ashburnham. Eventually, the Basil couple are transferred to Africa. Ashburnham then takes for his mistress the wife of a very young subordinate officer, Mrs. Maidan, who has a heart condition and accompanies the Ashburnhams to Bad Nauheim for treatment. On August 4, 1904, the day when the Dowells and the Ashburnhams first meet, Leonora has found Mrs. Maidan coming out of Ashburnham's bedroom in the hotel. Enraged, Leonora has slapped her and, in so doing, entangled her bracelet in Mrs. Maidan's hair. Florence Dowell, coming down the hallway, sees them struggling there and comes to help. Leonora lamely explains that she accidentally caught her bracelet in Mrs. Maidan's hair, and Florence helps them get untangled, as the sobbing Mrs. Maidan runs into her room. That evening, Leonora Ashburnham insists on sitting at the Dowell's dinner table in the hotel so as to forestall any gossip about that day's events. Mrs. Maidan soon dies, leaving Ashburnham free to form a liaison with Florence Dowell herself.

Ashburnham has an adoring ward, Nancy Rufford, a girl being educated in the same convent where Leonora went to school. As Nancy matures, Edward becomes attracted to her, but he is caught in a conflict between love and honor. He desires Nancy, but he is honor bound not to violate his sacred trust to protect her. Florence commits suicide when she learns suddenly that Ashburnham is attracted to Nancy and, at the same time, she is threatened with the revelation of her earlier infidelities. Ashburnham remains firm, however, and refuses to take advantage of his ward or corrupt her, even when she offers herself openly to him. He arranges for her to be sent to live with her father in Ceylon. On her voyage out, she cables Ashburnham from Brindisi a cheerful note implying that she feels no sorrow in leaving him. Ashburnham then commits suicide with a penknife. Nancy goes insane when she hears of his death. His widow, Leonora, marries a rabbit-like neighbor, Rodney Baynham, while Dowell is left the proprietor of the Branshaw Teleragh estate, tending the insane Nancy Rufford, now knowing that all the respectable decorum of the last nine years was merely a veneer over seething betrayal and infidelity.

The affair of *The Good Soldier* suggests the notion of saving or losing "face." Superficially, from the exterior, Edward Ashburnham has the "face" of the perfect ideal of the British officer class. He is compared in the text to the perfect knight, Chevalier Bayard, without fear and without reproach. He shows a resemblance to Christopher Tietjens in Ford's later tetralogy, superficially a model of the Anglican Tory landed gentry. Beneath his facade, however, the text indicates that his interior, deep personality is quite the contrary. He is a self-destructive raging stallion, ruining every female he meets, betraying all his companions to gratify his trivial desires. Ashburnham's exterior appearance of goodness masks his inner corruption.

All the major characters in *The Good Soldier* have two sides. Florence Dowell, the respectable wife, has had an affair with the contemptible Jimmy before her marriage. She may have trapped Dowell into marrying her simply so that she can get back to her lover in Europe. She certainly does not hesitate to become Ashburnham's mistress. She commits suicide when she learns that Ashburnham is attracted to his young ward and when she sees the man in whose house she committed adultery with Jimmy talking to her husband in their hotel. One of her motives for suicide is fear of losing face if her mask of respectability is torn away to reveal her hidden self.

Leonora Ashburnham, likewise, has her dark side hidden in a bright cloak of virtue. Although she is a sharp manager economically, she is cruel and unloving. The reader pities her husband.  Dowell, the narrator, too, is stupid, lazy, piggish, and deceitful, while claiming the applause due to virtue. He sometimes seems to tell lies intentionally, at other times unwittingly to fail to state the fictive "truth."  Since the work is fiction, the reader does not face a simple conflict between appearance and "reality," but between competing fictions. Is Ashburnham a noble knight or a despicable rake?  The story evaporates into conflicting impressions in Dowell's mind.

It could be seriously argued that Ashburnham, Leonora, Florence, and Nancy have no external "reality" at all, that they are simply the imaginings of the diseased mind of Dowell in his sickly dreams.  Compare the case of Robert Browning's "Porphyria's Lover." Browning's dramatic monologue is about the murder of a woman by her lover. The lover is the only witness and the sole reporter of the crime. Browning included this poem under the general heading, "From Madhouse Cells." Does Browning's imagined murderer, who tells us of his crime, report a fictive reality or should we take his words as a mad fantasy? Did Porphyria's lover "actually" kill the beloved, or is he merely imagining such a deed? Dowell's report similarly raises solipsistic questions. Is Dowell's report from a madhouse cell, a fantasy unconnected to any "real" event? Readers of conventional fiction may expect characters to be "real people," but all fictional characters are in a sense merely projections of the author's imagination. Ford's text, like Browning's, creates confusion about its conventional levels of reality.

In the "Dedicatory Letter" addressed to Stella Bowen in the head material for *The Good Soldier*, Ford quotes a critic as saying that *The Good Soldier* is "the finest French novel in the English language." Ford goes on to say that it was his ambition to do for the English novel what in *Fort comme la mort* (1889) Guy de Maupassant had done for the French. *Fort comme la mort* is the story of a society portrait painter, Olivier Bertin; Mme. de Guilleroy, his mistress; and Annette de Guilleroy, the young daughter of the mistress.

Bertin paints a striking portrait of Mme. de Guilleroy while she is dressed in mourning and over the years a deep and sincere love grows between them. When Annette de Guilleroy reaches marriageable age and comes to Paris, Bertin sees in the debutante a reincarnation of her mother as he first knew her. He is strongly attracted to the young girl, while the mother becomes obsessed with a fear of being compared to her daughter. When Annette's grandmother dies, she must wear mourning just as Mme. de Guilleroy did when Bertin first met her and painted her likeness. When Annette becomes engaged to a suitable young man, Bertin is so distracted and confused that he steps in front of an omnibus and is killed.

At first glance, there might seem to be some similarity in the plots of Ford's *The Good Soldier* and Maupassant's *Fort comme la mort.* In each the central male character feels a strong illicit attraction to a much younger girl who depends on him for protection: Ashburnham for Nancy Rufford, Bertin for Annette de Guilleroy. There are, however, many major differences between the two novels. For the most part, the plots are not comparable. In *Fort comme la mort* the older couple, Bertin and Mme de Guilleroy, are sincerely in love. The tension of the plot depends on the depth of that affection, disturbed by the resemblance of the young daughter to her mother. In *The Good Soldier*, Ashburnham and his wife are at daggers drawn. They do not speak to one another in private and Ashburnham receives no emotional support from his wife. His longing for the admiration and affection of Nancy is to fill a void.

Annette de Guilleroy is oblivious to the attraction she exerts toward Bertin. She is contentedly engaged to a young man appropriate to her own age. Nancy Rufford, on the other hand, knows of Ashburnham's affection and offers herself to him. Therefore the dilemma facing Ashburnham is different from that facing Bertin. Ashburnham has a conflict of love versus honor. He can physically possess the girl if he is willing to act dishonorably and violate his duty to protect his ward. Annette is physically out of Bertin's reach. His problem is that he loves the youthful image of Mme. de Guilleroy more than the aging woman herself.

A frequent topic in Maupassant is the "new woman," the independent or enfranchised intellectual female equal to male characters, who is complete mistress of her own passions. For example Maupassant's *Notre Coeur* (1890), a novel which displays the darkness of the heart as well as any text of Conrad's, opposes two women: On the one hand, the widow Mme. de Burne, who is the center of a highly intellectual Parisian salon, in control of her own destiny, but unable to make a full emotional commitment to her lover, Mariolle. On the other hand, Mariolle has the absolute, unquestioning devotion of a simple, vulnerable servant girl, Elizabeth. The novel shows his vacillation between the two types of women, in a dilemma similar to that of Edward Ashburnham in Ford's *The Good Soldier* caught between the steely mistress in Florence Dowell and the vulnerable, emotional girl in Nancy Rufford, whose love for him is headlong and without reservation.

Maupassant is the master of depicting "lost illusions." For example in *Une Vie,* the heroine Jeanne discovers that her husband has been unfaithful to her with her maid and with her best friend, that her own mother had committed adultery while maintaining an illusion of fidelity, that even her son betrays her. Finding her husband and best friend in a guilty tryst, Jeanne concludes:

> Tout le monde était donc, perfide, menteur, et faux . . . Elle se résolut pourtant à feindre de ne rien savoir (*Romans* 115).

> [Everyone was faithless, lying, false. She resolved to pretend not to know anything.]

Since everyone is pretending, the heroine is driven to pretense, to don a mask, to live disillusioned in the midst of illusions. The formula for the heroine's predicament in Maupassant's *Une Vie* resembles that of Dowell in Ford's *The Good Soldier.*

Maupassant's characterization, generally, provides a model for impressionist fiction. In *Pierre et Jean,* a dark brother competes with his fair-haired sibling. When an old friend of the family dies and leaves a large legacy to the younger, fair-haired man, his dark brother learns that their mother had committed adultery. The dark brother Pierre is described as a split character, embodying a man of feeling and a man of intellect. He is subject to feelings against which his intellect must struggle. So, when he first learns of his brother's inheritance, he feels jealousy and anger, despite himself:

> Il se mit à réfléchir profondément à ce problème physiologique de l'impression produite par un fait sur l'être instinctif et créant en lui un courant d'idées et de sensations douloureuses ou joyeuses, contraires à celles que désire, qu'appelle, que juge bonnes et saines l' être pensant (*Romans* 736).

> [He reflected deeply on this physiological problem of the impression produced by a stimulus on the responsive intelligence so as to create in it a current of ideas and feelings, painful or happy, contrary to what the thinking intelligence desires, calls for, or judges good and wholesome.]

All of Maupassant's stories involve some discontinuity of feeling and thought. Some stimulus calls up an emotional response unwanted by the rational mind.

When Ford suggests that he wants *The Good Soldier* to do for the English novel what Maupassant's *Fort comme la mort* did for the French, he seems to be thinking about characterization rather more than about turns of the plot. Mme. de Guilleroy, the matron, is confronted by Mme. de Guilleroy, the debutante, in the person of her daughter Annette. These two versions of the same character are brought together for Bertin's comparison, bewildering the aging lover. In his authorial voice, Maupassant steps into the last paragraph of Part I of *Fort comme la mort*, to discuss the characterization of Mme. De Guilleroy and Annette:

> De cette ressemblance naturelle et voulue, réelle et travaillée, était née dans l'esprit et dans le coeur du peintre l'impression bizarre d'un être double, ancien et nouveau, très connu et presque ignoré, de deux corps faits l'un après l'autre avec la même chair, de la même femme continuée, rajeunie, redevenue ce qu'elle avait été. Et il vivait près d'elles, partagé entre les deux, inquiet, troublé, sentant pour la mère ses ardeurs réveillées et couvrant la fille d'une obscure tendresse (*Romans* 919).

> [From this natural and willed resemblance, real and manufactured, there was born in the spirit and the heart of the painter the strange impression of a double being, the old and the young, well known and almost unknown, the impression of two bodies made one after the other of the same flesh, the same woman continued, made young again, become what she had been. And he lived beside them, divided between the two, turbulent, troubled, feeling his ardor for the mother reawakened and covering the daughter with an hidden tenderness.]

Maupassant records "l'impression bizarre" in Bertin's mind of an "être double," a doubled character in two versions: Annette and Mme. de Guilleroy. *The Good Soldier* might similarly be described as a record of the "bizarre impression" in the mind of Dowell, made by a doubled character in two versions: the bright public hero of Edward Ashburnham and his guilt-ridden dark inner twin. Dowell's observing intelligence—ironic, spiteful, macabre, full of incongruous comparisons and strange digressions—suggests the mind of Maupassant's painter/lover, Olivier Bertin, the keen reader of character in his portraits.

In *Fort comme la mort* Maupassant describes Bertin's mind:

> Il avait toujours eu l'esprit gouailleur, cette tendance française qui mêle une apparence d'ironie aux sentiments les plus sérieux . . . sans savoir saisir les distinctions subtiles des femmes, et discerner les limites des départements sacrés, comme il disait. (*Romans* 845)

> [He had always had a mocking spirit. The French tendency to mix an appearance of irony with the most serious sentiments . . . without being able to grasp the subtle distinctions of women and to perceive the limits of sacred grounds, as he would say.]

Dowell's intelligence, like Bertin's, supplies the "psychological reaction of one of the characters" which both Ford and Maupassant add to the "spectacle of the affair."

Ford's Dowell resembles Maupassant's Bertin in the extreme degree of their social alienation. Dowell's weariness and nausea appear on almost every page of *The Good Soldier*, "I asked myself unceasingly, my mind going round and round in a weary, baffled space of pain—what should these people have done? What in the name of God should they have done?" (264.03-06). The novel is about people who are physically and mentally sick, and Dowell is the sickest of the lot. He is passive and spiteful. He tells how he is filled with impatience and anxiety when the caviar is handed around "for fear that when the dish came to me there should not be a satisfying portion left over by the other guests" (52.11-12). Life for him is "a prison—a prison filled with screaming hysterics" (7.05-06). His weariness is overpowering: "I don't know. I know nothing. I am very tired" (278.12-13). The reader recognizes in the rising wail of Dowell the alien voice of modernist hysteria, the voice of T. S. Eliot's Prufrock or of Dostoyevsky's Underground Man.

In the concluding paragraph of *The March of Literature from Confucius to the Present Day,* Ford predicted "that the great work of art of the future will come from the fusion of the genius [for psychological analysis] of Dostoievsky with the art of impressionism" (ML 776). Fedor Mikhailovich Dostoyevsky (1821-81) in his *Notes from Underground* (1864) created a prototype of modernist alienation in the nauseated, frustrated, hidden, eccentric persona, for whom self-consciousness itself is a form of internal dialectical conflict. The Underground Man says to himself, "Now, I am living out my life in a corner, taunting myself with the spiteful and useless consolation that an intelligent man cannot become anything seriously, and it is only the fool who becomes anything. Yes, a man of the nineteenth century must and morally ought to be pre-eminently a characterless creature; a man of character, an active man, is pre-eminently a limited creature" (*Notes from Underground* 18). Dostoyevsky states one of Ford's major themes: the noble, vigorous, active, exceptional character is doomed in modern society because such characters are abnormal. They stand out in a crowd.

Modern warfare, like modern marriage and all other social institutions of the westernized modern world, works toward the homogenized, gray flannel-suited mass. In *The Good Soldier* Ford observes through Dowell,

> Conventions and traditions I suppose work blindly but surely for the preservation of the normal type; for the extinction of the proud, resolute, and unusual individuals. Edward was the normal man, but there was too much of the sentimentalist about him and society does not need too many sentimentalists. Nancy was a splendid creature but she had about her a touch of madness. Society does not need individuals with touches of madness about them. So Edward and Nancy were steamrolled out . . . (270.03-15)

The typical modern character, then, is part of a nightmare crowd of identical masks. Any spark of individuality must be repressed and hidden underground. Such a modernist anxiety is stated with particular force by Yevgeni Ivanovich Zamyatin (1884-1937) in his masterpiece *We* (1924) and repeatedly explored in works like Aldous Huxley's (1894-1963) *Brave New World* (1932) or George Orwell's (1903-1950) *1984* (1949). If Ford's *The Good Soldier* is the story of society's destruction of the too-generous, too-sentimental, good soldier Ashburnham; his Tietjens tetralogy similarly records modern society's rage against the exceptional Christopher Tietjens, too intelligent, too honest, too proud to survive in twentieth-century Europe.

In Ford's *Parade's End,* Christopher Tietjens foresees that there will be no place for him in England once World War I is over. He is too committed to the code of conduct which "Arnold forced upon Rugby" (PE 490). Tietjens asserts, "It is not good to have taken one's public school's ethical system seriously. I am really . . . the English public schoolboy . . . I remain adolescent" (PE 490). For this reason Tietjens is forever alienated from the postwar world: "I can never go home. I have to go underground somewhere. If I went back to England there would be nothing for me but going underground by suicide" (PE 491).

In *The Good Soldier* the spectacle of the destruction of the exceptional hero, Ashburnham, is reported through the eyes of Dowell so as to mount the psychological reaction of the passive, alienated Underground Man onto the visible affair. Dowell and Ashburnham have a startling inverse correspondence as if they were mirror images of each other or opposite numbers. Ashburnham is a man of action; Dowell is not. Ashburnham is everything a noble schoolboy hero should be: athletic, handsome, generous, fearless, the good soldier. Dowell is spiteful whenever he suspects that someone has been eating his caviar. Nevertheless, Dowell says explicitly and repeatedly that he and Ashburnham are the same man:

> Society can only exist if the normal, if the virtuous, and the slightly deceitful flourish, and if the passionate, the headstrong, and the too truthful are condemned to suicide and to madness. But I guess that I myself, in my fainter way, come into the category of the passionate, of the headstrong, and the too truthful. For I can't conceal from myself the fact that I loved Edward Ashburnham—and that *I loved him because he was just myself.* If I had the courage and the virility and possibly the physique of Edward Ashburnham I should, I fancy, have done much what he did. (emphasis supplied, 287.10-21)

Can it be that the strange impression of a double personality, *l'impression bizarre d'un être double,* in Maupassant's *Fort comme la mort* suggested to Ford the sad tale of Dowell who said he loved Ashburnham "because he was just myself"?

How is the reader to take the "truth value" of Dowell's equation of Ashburnham with himself, despite the obvious polar opposition of many of their traits? Perhaps Dowell is only speaking metaphorically? Or does Dowell speak literal truth when he equates himself with Ashburnham, as in Edgar Allen Poe's (1809-1849) short story "William Wilson," in which the hero is harried throughout life by a fellow who is a projection of his own conscience. The intervention of Dowell's intelligence between real reader and real author makes determining the "fictive truth" of any statement in the text difficult or, at best, merely a matter of artistic convention.

Should the reader believe that the events of *The Good Soldier* actually happened as reported by Dowell, or should the reader treat the text as a hallucination or fantasy produced by Dowell's unbalanced mind? Is the text a straightforward record of something that happened, or of something dreamed, a nightmare vision? Many spots in the text suggest that we are wrapped in Dowell's fantastic dream. After Florence commits suicide, Dowell says,

> I suppose that my inner soul,—my dual personality—had realized long before that Florence was a personality of paper—that she represented a real human being with a heart, with feelings, with sympathies, and with emotions only as a bank note represents a certain quantity of gold . . . I thought suddenly that she wasn't real; she was just a mass of talk out of guide-books, of drawings out of fashion plates. (138.09-20)

While the reader may nod assent, agreeing that the characters in this novel are all merely imaginary creations by Ford, made from scraps of remembered conversation, fashion plates, and guidebooks, in another sense the reader resists so privileging Dowell. The reader does not want to take Dowell as more real than Florence or Edward Ashburnham, so relegating them to merely hallucinatory status.

By channeling the events of *The Good Soldier* through the mind of Dowell, Ford intensifies the pathos of Ashburnham's destruction. Strained through the intellect of Dowell, the story becomes the joint tragedy of Dowell and Ashburnham. The outer-directed Dowell is linked to the inner-directed Ashburnham. Dostoyevsky's Underground Man sees that modern society destroys the strong, inner-directed heroes of the past, so he proposes his safety lies in giving up inner-direction, becoming characterless, going underground, denying his inner voice, and conforming to society's prescribed roles of behavior. Ford's text, by giving a simultaneous view of the fate of Ashburnham and the state of mind of Dowell, denies even the Underground Man's stratagem. The inner-directed hero appears crushed in Ashburnham's death, but the mental pain of the outer-directed, passive observer, Dowell, is equally unbearable. There is no exit.

Like Mme. de Guilleroy and Annette, Ashburnham and Dowell are an *être double*. Ford's pair of characters differs from Maupassant's because we see Ashburnham as he impinges on the mind of his counterpart, Dowell. Dowell tells the story of Ashburnham as it would be told if Mme. de Guilleroy were to report her psychological reaction to her encounter with her sexual rival fleshed in her uncanny mirror image in her daughter, Annette. Dowell and Ashburnham taken together, active versus passive, subject versus object, outer-directed versus inner-directed, represent the dilemma of modern alienation. Society destroys exceptional individuals, but a passive acceptance of society's enforced mediocrity is as horrible as destruction.

Dowell, like Dostoyevsky's Underground Man, alienated because modern society destroys the exceptional individual, more or less creates the good soldier, his fantasy of an outstanding hero in the character of Ashburnham. Ashburnham is to some degree a fantasy projected or distorted by Dowell's mind. Ashburnham's destruction is particularly meaningful as it is seen by Dowell because the two characters play out the dilemma of the modernist hero: the exceptional active man is steam rolled out, while the hidden passive observer is alienated. When literary impressionism mounts the "psychological reaction" of a character onto the "spectacle of the affair" in *The Good Soldier*, it enacts the dilemma of the modernist divided self. At one pole of the split modernist hero is the pained paralysis of an ironic observer like Prufrock and at the opposite pole is the farewell to arms of the doomed and outdated warrior hero. By mounting the psychological reaction of Dowell onto the spectacle of Ashburnham's affair, the impressionist text reintegrates the split between observer and agent.

# CHAPTER II
## IMPRESSIONIST VERBAL COLLAGE

*Manipulation of Point of View: Limited, "Unreliable," Eccentric. Collage: Fragmentation, Defamiliarization, Juxtaposition, Incrementation. Selection of Detail. Constructive Activity of Audience. Cinematic Structures. Henri Bergson's Duration.*

Ford claimed that he and Conrad developed the notion that the novel must be a rendering of impressions, not a narration, and that the subject matter for the novel must always be an *affair* involving a network of human roles shifting under the stress of an unusual pressure. This kind of a story diverts the reader's attention from its nominal subject to the perceiving intellect of the story teller or observer comprehending and shaping that material, so as to mount a "psychological reaction" onto the "spectacle of the affair." Attention shifts from events and characters in the tale to the way the events strike the story teller and how the story teller shapes the text. The principle of verisimilitude of the naive realist (to reflect accurately in art the phenomena of the world) becomes, rather, that of the impressionist (to represent a mind in the act of experiencing the outer world).

"Turn of the Screw" by Henry James, for example, is an impressionist narrative because it depicts not merely a sequence of events in Castle Bly in which little Miles and Flora act; but, rather more importantly, it also displays the mind of the Governess, possibly going mad, as she sees those events and shapes them into her mental fabric of guilt and anxiety. Her "impression," her psychological reaction, is mounted onto the spectacle of the affair presented by the actions and events she reports.

When the writer shifts attention from the events perceived to the act of perception, it follows that there must be a corresponding development of limited point of view, of non-linear narrative time structures, and of mental space into nightmare worlds replacing topographic realism. Language must be employed not merely to make a statement about experience, but to be a model of the act of experiencing.

In *Joseph Conrad: A Personal Remembrance* Ford exemplifies the construction of an impressionist novel in his facetious history of Mr. Slack:

> We agreed that the general effect of a novel must be the general effect that life makes on Mankind. A novel must therefore not be a narration, a report. Life does not say to you: In 1914 my next door neighbor, Mr. Slack, erected a greenhouse and painted it with Cox's green aluminum paint . . . If you think about the matter you will remember, in various and unordered pictures, how one day Mr. Slack appeared in his garden and contemplated the wall of his

house. You will then try to remember the year of that occurrence and you will fix it as August 1914 because having had the foresight to bear the municipal stock of the city of Liege you were able to afford a first class season ticket for the first time in your life . . . (JC 180-81)

and so on, for several pages, Ford follows the twisting thought processes of his narrator.

Ford calls this sort of story "impressionism" because "life did not narrate, but made impressions on our brains" and so the writer must "render impressions" in order to be true to life. When Ford depicts Conrad himself in his memoir, he uses such patterns of associative indirection to characterize Conrad while at the same time claiming that he and Conrad invented and employed these conventions during their collaboration.

The modern reader, who has struggled with works such as John Barth's *The Sot-weed Factor* (1960), Thomas Pynchon's *Gravity's Rainbow* (1973), or Robert Coover's *Pricksongs and Descants* (1969), recognizes in Ford's position very serious implications about the structure of time and space in everyday reality, as well as in fictional narratives. The limited central intelligence, generating its stream of consciousness, holds in layers levels of remembered past, fictive present, and fantasized future. The impressionist narrative resembles a palimpsest, or sheet of parchment which has been repeatedly written over. Since parchment was an expensive medium to carry writing, a single sheet might be used initially perhaps for a legal document, then partially erased years later to be re-used for a personal letter, and later still perhaps for a memorandum, so that the modern historian can decipher various levels of signification dimly visible, but simultaneously present, on a single surface. Such a palimpsest resembles the superimposed scheme of layers of time in impressionist narratives like Ford's *The Good Soldier*.

The mental activity of the impressionist narrator fragments reality and "defamiliarizes" everyday occurrences by setting them in new and unexpected contexts. When a character is pinned down by an artillery barrage at the French front in World War I, as Christopher Tietjens is upon occasion in Ford's Tietjens Tetralogy, his immediate sensations need not be particularly prominent. As Ford noted:

> Your thoughts were really concentrated on something quite distant: on your daughter Millicent's hair, on the fall of the Asquith ministry, on your financial predicament, on why your regimental ferrets kept on dying, on whether Latin is really necessary to an education, or in what way really *ought* the authorities to deal with certain diseases . . . You were there, but great shafts of thought from the outside, distant and unattainable world infinitely for the greater part occupied your mind. (JC 192)

Ford imagines the central intelligence bringing a host of apparently unrelated questions to the immediate situation. The intelligence asks the questions which define the "reality" of the scene. "Reality" is not just the hail of physical projectiles on the battlefield. The arena is mental, where warring concerns, transfixed shafts of thought, painfully intersect in layered consciousness. Some stimuli are judged "important" and registered, others are suppressed as trivial and go unmarked.

The questions asked by the mind determine what the consciousness registers. The mind functions as a screening device, eliminating "unimportant" details until it can see some meaningful pattern in the mass of events flowing past it. The mind asks the questions which screen out the non-significant, or make the conception of *non-significant* possible. What we view as reality is the mediation between the cognitive frame brought to experience by the mind and the sensory stimulation provided to the senses by an "outer" world.

"Selection" is therefore a major technical feature of impressionist fiction, especially as it produces what Ford calls in *The March of Literature from Confucius to Modern Times* the "unearned increment":

> Impressionism began with the—perhaps instinctive—discovery . . . that the juxtaposition of the composed renderings of two or more unexaggerated actions or situations may be used to establish, like the juxtaposition of vital word to vital word, a sort of frictional current of electric life that will extraordinarily galvanize the work of art in which the device is employed . . . The point cannot be sufficiently labored, since the whole fabric of modern art depends on it. (ML 734)

Ford commends specifically Flaubert's exploitation of this "unearned increment" in scenes such as the seduction of Emma Bovary by Rodolphe at the agricultural fair. The romantic pair are secluded behind a window overlooking the speaker's platform so that their private conversation is superimposed on the agricultural awards ceremony. In this well-known scene, we recall that Rodolphe's seductive advances are interlaced by the stentorian announcements of the prizes. At the climax of Rodolphe's courting, the announcer cries out the prize for *"fumiers"* [*"manure"*]. This is a funny scene because of the juxtaposition of two logically unconnected speeches which are not in themselves comic. By the non-logical juxtaposition, the president's utterance, *manure*, is made to comment on Rodolphe's gallant lie to Emma about his fidelity. The implication is not merely that Rodolphe's character is excremental but also that the process depicted is one of cultivation. Like a good farmer, Rodolphe is working a productive field in Emma's character which he hopes will yield a return for his efforts. When she responds favorably to his advances, the president awards a duplicate prize for swine ("race porcine, *prix ex aequo*").

This rather crude effect of direct commentary between the two speeches, each from widely differing arenas of action, is only a symptom of the broad juxtaposition which lies at the center of Flaubert's *Madame Bovary*—the juxtaposition of the romantic notions of Emma with the "productive" daily life in provincial Yonville. The force and vitality of the novel as a whole resides primarily in such juxtaposition. Emma's romantic conduct is shown to be self-destructive in this context, but there is a strong current in the work running counter to that moral indictment and enlisting the reader's sympathy for Emma. This tension between sympathy and judgment is apparent in the seduction scene. As Emma yields to Rodolphe's arguments and clutches his hand, there is no question but that she must be judged morally wrong and on the path to ruin. But at that moment, below, a silver medal for fifty-four years of continuous work is awarded to the woman Catherine Leroux. After much hustling and confusion, the poor old woman is thrust forward to receive her prize and is depicted as brutalized by her years of labor.

Here are juxtaposed the faithful servant and the unfaithful wife, logically unconnected but commenting one upon the other. Rodolphe and Emma may be acting like swine, but fidelity alone as personified in Catherine Leroux is equally brutalizing. And so, while judging Emma morally wrong, the reader sympathizes with Emma's dissatisfaction and longing for an escape from the fate of Catherine Leroux, which is the public role offered her by the provincial society of Yonville. Emma's tragic dilemma is that both roles open to her, middle class faithful wife versus aristocratic adventuress, are unfulfilling and destructive. In her private personality, she can accept neither role fully.

Neither the agricultural fair nor the seduction itself are funny when considered alone, only when they are brought into juxtaposition do they produce laughter in the way they comment on each other. Likewise the tragic statement of the text resides in the clash of juxtaposed roles open to Emma. As Ford maintains, juxtaposition vitalizes the text.

Conrad maintained that there was a close connection between his own creative effort and Flaubert's. Part of that posture involved asserting that he had begun to write his first novel on the blank pages of his copy of *Madame Bovary*. Ford cheerfully accepts and elaborates this improbable testimony as proof of a line connecting Conrad and Flaubert intellectually. In *The March of Literature from Confucius to Modern Times*, Ford notes that Conrad's first novel *Almayer's Folly* was begun by one of the

> Coincidence[s] . . . the most curious in literary history—on the margins and
> end papers of *Madame Bovary* whilst his ship was moored to the dockside in
> Rouen harbour, and the portholes of his cabin there gave a view of the house
> which Flaubert described as being the meeting place of Emma Bovary and
> Rodolphe. That would be in 1893. (ML 766)

Ford, as biographer of Conrad, in this passage is probably deviating wildly from historical fact. The reason for his deviation is clear: he sees Flaubert and Conrad as successive steps in the "march" of literature toward literary impressionism. In that march, it is only a step from the incremental juxtapositions of *Madame Bovary*, trying to play conflicting roles in order simultaneously to please herself and to satisfy the morality of bourgeois society, to the pattern of associations in Marlow's recollection of Lord Jim's career.

Recall Marlow's first meeting with Jim, outside the Court of Inquiry in an Eastern port. The affair under scrutiny concerns how the badly damaged pilgrim ship Patna was abandoned at sea by its officers so as to leave its passengers to their fate. As Marlow and Jim leave the crowded building, there is a native dog sneaking in the way. Someone says, "look at that wretched cur" (83.27). Jim turns toward Marlow and asks, "Did you speak to me?" From that hostile beginning, based on the misconception that Marlow had called him a "wretched cur," Jim accepts Marlow's invitation to dine at Malabar House and so begins to tell his tale. Emma Bovary's affair with Rodolphe is not merely "*fumiers*" and Lord Jim is not merely a "wretched cur," although those pairs of ideas are juxtaposed in the text so as to produce a grim laughter. Both Flaubert and Conrad grasp the power of juxtaposition to create laughter and tears.

Incremental juxtaposition is a common feature of poetic discourse. For example in Ford's "What the Orderly Dog Saw" from *On Heaven and Other Poems* these poignant lines owe their effect to associative juxtaposition of details:

> The seven white peacocks against the castle wall
> In the high trees and the dusk are like tapestry
> The sky being orange, the high wall a purple barrier.
> The canal, dead silver in the dusk,
> And you are far away.
> Yet I can see infinite miles of mountains.
> Little lights shining in rows in the dark of them;
> Infinite miles of marshes.
> Thin wisps of mist, shimmering like blue webs
> Over the dusk of them, great curves and horns of sea
> And dusk and dusk and the little village
> And you, sitting in the firelight.
> Around me are the two hundred and forty men of B company
> Mud-colored.
> Going about their avocations,
> Resting between their practice of the art
> Of killing men,
> As I too rest between my practice
> Of the art of killing men.
> Their pipes glow above the mud and their mud color.
> Moving like fireflies beneath the trees . . .

"Orderly Dog" in the military parlance of World War I signifies "O. D." or "Officer of the Day." These lines register what the Officer of the Day sees directly, as a camera eye, juxtaposed with what he remembers from contrasting peacetime.

In the first stanza, the speaker looks up to the castle wall and describes his impressions; in the second stanza, the speaker drops his eyes to the plain and describes his impressions of that contrasting setting. The first twelve lines refer to one scene, its impressions and the memories evoked by those stimuli. It has an emotional tone of calm nostalgia. The next nine lines describing the soldiers have a completely different effect, but when these two renderings are placed side by side they intensify each other. The nostalgia of the first part becomes much more poignant through its juxtaposition with the later war scene. Such increased poignancy or sharpened emotional statement is what Ford called the unearned increment. The two impressions taken together mean much more than when considered separately.

Ford's theory of impressionist narrative reflects the idea of artistic collage, with its four key processes: fragmentation, defamiliarization, juxtaposition, and incrementation. In *The March of Literature from Confucius to Modern Times* Ford asserts that the whole fabric of modern art depends on the discovery that juxtaposition of disparate actions, situations, and details will galvanize a work of art. Unexpected juxtaposition, like a current of electricity, brings to life the tangled web of associations which make the fabric of impressionist narratives.

The collage pastes or glues together disparate elements into a   coherent artistic organization, for example as in Pablo Picasso's "Le Rêve" (1908), Carlo Carra's "Patriotic Celebration" (1914), Kurt Schwitters's "Picture with a Light Center" (1919), George Grosz's "The Engineer Heartfield" (1920), or Richard Hamilton's "Just What Is It That Makes Today's Homes So Different, So Appealing?" (1956). Each of these images is created by gluing together fragments taken from alien contexts. The artist first extracts a fragment from its normal context, for example by tearing a strip from a newspaper or from an advertisement. Fragmented bits of reality thus become "defamiliarized" and the viewer is compelled to look "harder," to pay attention to qualities in the fragment which might normally be taken for granted or overlooked, if it stood in its usual context. The defamiliarized fragments are then pasted together in a new configuration, in a fresh and unexpected juxtaposition, so as to create an incremented total meaning far greater than the meanings of the fragments considered separately. Ford's impressionist texts form verbal collages similarly.

Pablo Picasso's "Le Rêve" (1908) depicts a set of anthropomorphic, nude, female, cubist figures in ink forming a frame inside of which is pasted a separate fragment of paper showing a male figure in a boat. To readers accustomed to the framed tales of Conrad, like "Heart of Darkness" or *Lord Jim*, the collage by Picasso raises familiar questions about levels of reality. Do the anthropomorphic ink figures in the outer framing scene dream the vision of the boat, or does the figure in the boat imagine the idyllic setting of the frame? Of course, since both parts of the picture are equally products of the artist's mind, the interesting question is not, "Which part of the picture is real and which imaginary?" but, "Why does the viewer feel compelled to divide this picture into two levels of reality when both the frame and the central scene are equally imaginary?" The juxtaposition of outer frame and inner scene forces the viewer into a constructive activity, "reading" or judging how the fragments in the collage connect and classifying the parts in a hierarchy of "more real" versus "less real." In Ford's *The Good Soldier* a similar tension exists about the levels of reality of Dowell the storyteller versus agents like Edward Ashburnham, Florence, and Leonora. Are the agents perhaps merely a dream or fantasy generated by Dowell, or do they stand on the same level of reality as the story teller?

The introduction of the collage as a form into Picasso's work marks the end of the early or "analytic" phase of cubism, in which the artist tries simply to break natural shapes into their elementary components; and begins synthetic cubism, which builds larger structures from elementary forms, for example Picasso's "Three Musicians" (1921). Here the collage introduces materials such as newspaper clippings torn from their contexts in real life, so that the reality of the fragmentary parts of the picture is contrasted and counter pointed against the artificial abstraction of the larger organizing design, the three human figures, created by the artist's arrangement of the various pieces.

In "Three Musicians" Picasso positions multi-colored fragments of scrap paper so as to suggest quite strongly three anthropomorphic, clownesque human shapes: one on the left in parti-colored dress suggesting harlequin with a violin bow in his hand, the central figure in white seated behind a page of music, and the dark figure on the right with a keyboard. All seem to be masked, and our recognition of these shapes as human is based on the artist's quite sketchy suggestion. If, for example, we screen off the upper half of the picture, we do not recognize the shapes in the lower half as knees, legs, and feet. What we see are angular geometric shapes in flat planes with sharply contrasting colors. We need the total picture to be able to "read" it as representational, unlike a scene by Fragonard in which a flashing ankle revealed amidst a whirl of flowing cloth could never be mistaken for merely a geometric shape. In Picasso's picture, the constituent parts pull against the organizing force of his over all representational design so that the parts threaten to "run away" with the meaning, dissolving the anthropomorphic, human reference into mere shapes.

The struggle or tension between fragmentary detail and the overall organizing design accounts for the impact of works like Carlo Carra's collage "Patriotic Celebration (Free Word Painting)" (1914). This picture is composed of fragments cut from newspapers and magazines with words and letters in varied typefaces printed on multi-colored papers in colorful inks. The fragments are arranged in a vortex, or spiraling pattern, so that the pieces seem to blast outward from a center. The ordering power of the artist's abstract spiral design holds the whirling fragments in place, like a center of human consciousness just barely in control of the barrage of information pounding in on it in day-to-day life. In Picasso's "Le Rêve" there is a significant tension between the frame of luxuriating nudes and the fisherman in the central panel. In Carra's "Patriotic Celebration" the opposition is not between frame and core, but between the incoherent fragments and the ordering power of the overlying formal organization.

In the tension between its elements, the assemblage makes a statement far greater than its individual parts considered separately. Photomontage in the cinema frequently demonstrates this incremented statement. In the 1960's an ephemeral street poster opposed to the war in Viet Nam appeared, showing two photographs superimposed as if in a double exposure: one image showed a modern industrial assembly line; the other a burning Asiatic baby. The collage implies a relation between its elements. In the case of this anti-war poster, the relationship is causal. The picture accuses capitalist industry of causing Asian babies to burn, even though that accusation is nowhere explicitly stated. In a similar way, the viewer tries to "read" a relation among the parts of Picasso's "Le Rêve," instinctively subordinating one part to the other so that the frame figures "dream" the central picture or the boatman "imagines" the surrounding nudes.

The very act of making a collage constitutes a criticism of the initial organization of its materials in their real-life situations. When actual pieces are torn out of everyday life to be organized into an artifact, the work of art becomes a criticism of the confusion, disorder, ugliness, and stereotyped attitudes in the initial, real environment from which the fragment is detached. The work of art offers an alternative way of seeing this particular bit of reality. In Richard Hamilton's "Just What Is It That Makes Today's Homes So Different, So Appealing?" fragments taken perhaps from commercial advertising illustrations come together in one horrible modern environment inhabited by Charles Atlas and Marilyn Monroe. By actually incorporating into the picture pieces of modern life, the artist's work directs strong criticism against the vulgarity of commercial images surrounding us. The collage assembles its parts in such a way that the viewer is faced with two or more conflicting versions of reality, a "double take" on the material.

The verbal collage is a key element in Ford's idea of literary impressionism. In *Joseph Conrad: A Personal Remembrance* Ford asserts that a novel should not narrate, but "render impressions." It must proceed by associative indirection, locked in the limitations of a central intelligence whose struggle for understanding is the main concern to the reader. The writer must mount the "psychological reaction" of a character onto the "spectacle of the affair." To illustrate impressionist style, Ford constructs a lengthy, facetious example showing how the saga of a certain Mr. Slack should (and should not) be written. Life does not say to you, "In 1914 my next door neighbor, Mr. Slack, erected a green house and painted it with Cox's green aluminum paint." The novel, if it is to render the process of real consciousness must shift the focus of that scene in this way:

> If you think about the matter you will remember, in various and unordered pictures . . . Mr. Slack—then much thinner because it was before he found out where to buy that cheap Burgundy of which he has since drunk an inordinate quantity though whiskey you think would be much better for him! Mr. Slack again came into his garden, this time with a pale, weaselly-faced fellow, who touched his cap from time to time. Mr. Slack will point to his housewall several times at different points, the weaselly fellow touching his cap at each pointing. Some days after, coming back from business you will remember that you were then manager of the fresh-fish branch of Messrs. Catlin and Clovis in Fenchurch Street . . . What a change since then! Millicent had not yet put her hair up . . . You will remember how it now looks, henna'd: and you will see in one corner of your mind's eye a little picture of Mr. Mills the vicar talking— oh, very kindly—to Millicent after she had come back from Brighton . . . But perhaps you had better not risk that. You remember some of the things said by means of which Millicent has made you cringe—and her expression! . . . Cox's Aluminum Paint! . . . You remember the half empty tin that Mr. Slack showed you—he had a most undignified cold—with the name in a horse-shoe over a blue circle that contained a red lion asleep in front of a real-gold sun . . . (JC 192-3)

Such a passage shows a structural similarity to the visual collages of Picasso, Carra, Grosz, Schwitters, and Hamilton and it is typical of many passages in Ford's best fiction as well.

Compare, for instance, the concluding paragraphs of Ford's *A Man Could Stand Up*, depicting a drunken post-war celebration as seen by Valentine Wannop. Valentine has just decided that she will abandon traditional inhibitions and become the mistress of Christopher Tietjens. She is surrounded by revelers on Armistice Day, who are shouting out a popular song from World War I, while Valentine prepares to enter a new life with Christopher:

> "Over here! Pom Pom! Over here! Pom Pom! That's the word that's the word; Over here . . . " At least they weren't over there! They were prancing. The whole world around them was yelling and prancing round. They were the centre of unending roaring circles. The man with the eyeglass has stuck a half-crown in his other eye. He was well-meaning. A brother. She had a brother with the V.C. All in the family. Tietjens was stretching out his two hands from the waist. It was incomprehensible. His right hand was behind her back, his left in her right hand. She was frightened. She was amazed. Did you ever! He was swaying slowly. The elephant! They were dancing!

Aranjuez was hanging on to the tall woman like a kid on a telegraph-pole. The officer who had said he had picked up a little bit of fluff . . . well, he had! He had run out and fetched it. It wore white-cotton gloves and a flowered hat. It said: "Ow! Now! . . . " There was a fellow with a most beautiful voice. He led: better than a gramophone. Better . . . Les petites marionettes, font! font! font! . . . On an elephant. A dear, meal-sack elephant. She was setting out on . . . (PE 674)

The visualization of Tietjens as a sad sack elephant brings to mind Max Ernst's (1891-1976) painting *Celebes* (1921), now in the Tate Gallery in London, which is often asserted to be the beginning point of surrealism in modernist painting. Ernst creates his image by bringing together normally unrelated objects in settings which are inappropriate for them in our ordinary experience, so exploiting the process of defamiliarization and juxtaposition. In this canvas he constructs an ungainly mechanical monster from parts of what appears to be a gas mask, vacuum sweeper, or perhaps a hydraulic pump. This awkward mechanism clearly suggests an enormous elephant. In the foreground right corner there is a headless female nude figure gesturing dramatically. Both elephant and wounded female are set in a gray waste land, perhaps devastated by war, with smoky clouds above a flat, low horizon, with two broken metallic structures rising at the right and left edge of the landscape. In the upper right corner in the dark sky there is what might be a small airplane, World War I vintage, being shot down, spiraling in flames. The elephant might be a military tank on the runway of a strafed air field, but for the nude headless female gesturing.

Ernst believed that the structure of such surrealist images exhibits an associative power similar to that which Freud found in dreams. Ernst's painting is at once frightening, recalling the horrors which Ernst had personally experienced in World War I, and grotesquely funny, as the bewildered, mechanical, clumsy elephant peers obtusely from its single eye. It is said that Ernst associated this image with the schoolboy doggerel taunt: "the elephant from Celebes/ with sticky yellow bottom grease."

Not only does Ford's image of Tietjens as elephant mount the eccentric psychological reaction of Valentine onto the spectacle of the affair at the party so that her mental processes, associated memories, and immediate impressions blend into a verbal palimpsest; but also the basic structural principles of the collage come into play in the text with fragmentation, defamiliarization, and juxtaposition forcing the reader into a highly constructive activity to deduce the relationship among the whirling fragments. The implied incremented statement is the simultaneous confusion, distress, hope, and disorientation of Valentine as she is about to depart on her new, postwar, unpredictable life with her ungainly lover, like the headless nude motioning the elephant of the Celebes forward in Ernst's surreal landscape.

In the verbal collage concluding *A Man Could Stand Up*, Valentine is at the "centre of unending roaring circles," in an environment where World War I has destroyed the religious, patriotic, and social order. In that chaos of alcohol, sex, violence, and incoherence, she clings to Christopher to give meaning and order to her life. The primary concern of the reader is her mental state: her confusion, her distress, and her hopes. Ford has mounted her psychological reaction onto the spectacle of the affair: the man with the half-crown eyeglass, her brother with a Victoria Cross (or is it a Venereal Crisis), the man dancing with the tall woman like a kid hanging on a telephone pole, the bit of fluff who speaks with a cockney accent, and the elephantine Tietjens himself. Her mind organizes these whirling elements into a hope for the future, her elephant, which will carry her through. That process modeled in her stream of consciousness is imitated in the constructive activity of the reader, who is also confronted with whirling images, shifting levels of reality, and fragments defamiliarized in strange contexts. The power of the fiction is that the reader's activity parallels the activity of the fictive central intelligence in searching for a controlling pattern which will hold together these detached fragments of experience. The reader experiences the tension of the observer.

Kurt Schwitters made collages from pieces of advertisements and discarded packaging materials from mass produced, commercial goods. He called these collages "Merzbilder," suggesting in the French word "merde" his contempt for modern mass production, high consumption society. He also had in mind the German word for "commerce." The fragments making his collage come from a commercial setting, but are put to an unexpected aesthetic use in his art. The initial act of tearing fragments from the real world, or picking up pieces of garbage churned out by commerce, implies that the organization of everyday life is falling apart, the center does not hold. Religion, patriotism, family, the marketplace, all the traditional sources of order and value lose their power to provide meaning in the modern world and we are all swept along in a meaningless whirl of events, images, words, and junk. Only the activity of the artist can bring coherence and form to the fragmentary world around us. The creation of the collage criticizes the incoherence of modern popular culture. Schwitters therefore reinforces one of the basic myths of modernist ideology, that the modern world is falling into chaos and requires an artist to restore its organizing structures, which is a central ideological assumption in Ford's *Joseph Conrad: A Personal Remembrance* and *The March of Literature from Confucius to Modern Times*.

When Ford claims in *Joseph Conrad: A Personal Remembrance* that the whole fabric of modern art depends on juxtaposition, putting side by side two elements to galvanize the work of art and increment its statement, he is not simply claiming that the work as a whole means more than its parts taken separately. Confronted with artistic juxtaposition, the reader is forced to infer relations among the parts.

The power of the artifact resides in its ability to generate this activity in the audience. When a work of art merely reflects an exterior reality, we usually call it realistic. When it expresses a state of mind either of the artist or of an imagined character, we call it expressive. The audience responds to realist and to expressive art in a passive way. The audience does not contribute to the creation of the realist or of the expressive artifact, it merely responds to the work of art. But juxtaposed renderings require more than a passive response. Ford's idea of impressionism requires the audience to participate actively in creating the artifact while in the process of experiencing it.

In an impressionist text, the reader will be at first confused and disoriented by the defamiliarization of its fragmentary parts detached from their normal, everyday contexts. Normal landmarks for the reader in space, time, and causality will be missing. The artifact will pose questions about levels of reality: What part of the text is fictive "reality," what dream, nightmare, or hallucination? What is the relation of frame to core in Picasso's "Le Rêve," James's *Turn of the Screw*, or Conrad's "Heart of Darkness"?

The audience is called upon to construct for itself from the fragmentary stimuli of the text an overall design unifying the work of art. The verbal collage operates like the pointillist colors in Seurat, when the canvas juxtaposes dots of yellow with dots of blue pigment which merge only on the retina of each viewer's eye in an optical mixture of intense green. Such an optical mixture of color is like the intense political statement created by the photo-montage in the Viet Nam era poster of an assembly line superimposed on a burning Asian baby, described above. The real flash of color or of understanding occurs in the perceptive mind and it is created by the constructive participation of the viewer creating the artifact. When the observing intelligence "puts two and two together," it creates an incremented meaning greater than the explicit meaning of the individual parts of the collage.

The verisimilitude which Ford demands in a novel is a true representation of a mind at work on the chaos of impressions it receives and the welter of associated memories through which it must proceed. A novel which has verisimilitude for Ford truly records the processes of ratiocination. For this reason *The Good Soldier* is not written in chronological sequence. It represents the reverie of Dowell. It shows the story teller's mind at work and the text must follow the order in which Dowell's mind would proceed.

An examination of the monologues of the Tietjens Tetralogy shows Ford striving for impressionist verisimilitude by following the laws of mental association formulated by the great impressionist philosopher, David Hume (1711-76). Hume in his *Philosophical Essays: Concerning Human Understanding* (1748) maintained that all objects of human reason or inquiry can be divided into matters of fact, or *ideas* which are memories of direct sensory impressions, and the *relations* between such ideas. Ideas are related in the mind through resemblance, contiguity, or cause and effect.

The transitions in limited narration in Ford's fiction are built on Hume's principles governing the association of ideas.    For instance, Mark's first monologue in *The Last Post* begins with a simple record of fact:

> Old Gunning lumbered slowly up the path towards the stable, his hands swinging. The stable was a tile heeled affair . . .

It did not *resemble* a northern stable.

> No real stable in the north country sense—a place where the old mare sheltered among the chickens and ducks . . .

*because*

> There was no tidiness amongst the south country folks. They hadn't it in them . . .

They did not *resemble* Gunning.

> Though Gunning could bind a tidy thatch and trim a hedge properly. All round man. Really an all round man . . .

*because*

> He could do a great many things. He knew all about fox hunting, pheasant rearing, wood-craft, hedging, dyking, pig rearing, and the habits of King Edward when shooting.

The *contiguity* of the idea of King Edward suggests the fact that King Edward has been seen,

> Smoking endless great cigars! One finished, light another, throw away the stub.

The *contiguity* of fox hunting and King Edward suggests

> fox hunting, the sport of kings with only twenty percent of the danger of war (PE 678).

In such passages the reader must construct the connection between fragmented, broken sequences of images in imitation of the mental associations of the limited dramatic persona who utters the language.

Verbal collages not only utilize the juxtaposition of fragments of reality to create an emotional increment, they also force the reader into an unusually active role. The reader must follow the chronology of explanation and deduce the significance of details. The real point of the total statement is created within the mind of each reader. Flaubert simply sets Rodolphe's courting and a prize for manure together. The reader makes the connection between the two, which is nowhere stated explicitly in the text. The reader creates the fabric of the text, its network of connections, from fragmentary suggestions. Such a highly constructive role of the reader is like the constructive participation of the viewer before a pointillist canvas by Seurat.

When a viewer stands before a painting by Seurat, what is actually before the eyes is a pointillist configuration of dots of color, but on the retina of the viewer's eye these dots flow together into an optical mixture so that each observer constructs the picture afresh, seeing colors and shapes that are not on the canvas at all. Color for the pointillist is a form of optical illusion. For an impressionist author, the text likewise is only a stimulus to generate in each reader a construction.

Recall the beginning of Chapter II of Conrad's "Heart of Darkness." Marlow has been working to repair his river steamer which was sunk before his arrival at the inner station in the Congo. His mission is to take that ship up river to rescue the agent Kurtz. Marlow knows nothing about Kurtz except that he is said to be of the party of high principles, who justify the European invasion of Africa as a step toward civilization, and that he has sent large shipments of ivory down river.

Compare this scene from "Heart of Darkness" to the agricultural fair in *Madame Bovary*: Marlow is dozing at night on the deck of his ship. He hears voices approaching. He recognizes the manager of the inner station and his nephew. They walk back and forth along the bank, just below Marlow's head, talking without knowing that he is listening. Marlow represents an eccentric point of view, positioned just above the line of sight of the speakers as they walk along the dock below him in the darkness. Marlow is at first so drowsy that he is inattentive; but, when he recognizes that they are talking about Kurtz, he comes fully awake.

The uncle and his nephew stroll in and out of earshot so that Marlow hears only broken fragments of their conversation:

> "Military post—doctor—two hundred miles—quite alone now—unavoidable delays—nine months—no news—strange rumors." They approached again, just as the manager was saying, "No one, as far as I know, unless a species of wandering trader—pestilential fellow, snapping ivory from the natives." Who was it they were talking about now? . . . They moved off and whispered, then their voices rose again. "The extra-ordinary series of delays is not my fault. I did my best." The fat man sighed. "Very sad." "And the pestiferous absurdity of his talk," continued the other; "he bothered me enough when he was here." "Each station should be like a beacon on the road towards better things, a centre for trade of course, but also for humanizing, improving, instructing." "Conceive you—that ass! And he wants to be manager! No, it's—"Here he got choked by excessive indignation, and I lifted my head the least bit. I was surprized to see how near they were—right under me." (90-1)

In such a passage, Conrad fragments his sentences and uses Marlow's eccentric center of consciousness to force the reader into the activity of constructing a meaning for the scene. The reader must replicate the manner in which Marlow grapples with fragmentary clues. The reader's chronology of understanding is like Marlow's, but has a pace of its own. Marlow seems at times quite obtuse, so that he shows us more than he understands. In this case, the reader has no trouble deducing from the fragments of conversation that the manager of the inner station is Kurtz's enemy and that the manager hopes for the destruction of Kurtz while he is marooned up river. The reader who already knows the full text will see an inner irony that Kurtz, the man of "principle," has turned even more vicious isolated in the heart of Africa than the unprincipled manager.

Although we can never know certainly why Conrad wrote this scene in such a fragmentary and indirect way, Ford apparently identified such scenes as a step in an artistic movement which later flourished in Faulkner, Joyce, Rhys, and Ford's own best work.

The perceiving intellect, the limited point of view, organizes and screens the material stated in this scene, so that we hear only what Marlow hears and see only what he sees. Juxtaposition of past memory, fantasy, and fictive present impressions are made in his mind. Most readers of Conrad would agree that such mental collages are typical of the indirect narration of Marlow. Not only is the texture of juxtaposed images held in Marlow's mind, but Marlow's consciousness also makes possible the broad juxtaposition in "Heart of Darkness" between the comfortable yacht where the story teller Marlow tells his tale on the river Thames versus his journey into the "primitive" remembered horrors of the African Congo. Only the mind of this story teller can bring the remembered past and fictive present together and weave the story associatively from Europe to the Congo, following his stream of thought.

Many of the narrative conventions valued by Ford appear to be prototypes for the cinema. The rapid juxtaposition of still frames projected from the reel of cinema film blurs in the optical resolution on the retinas of the audience into an illusion of motion. The movie we see is an illusion created in the eyes of the beholder. The cinema claims at once an intimate connection with reality, because the scene must be a photograph of some real object, yet it creates its art by distortion through eccentric point of view, fluid time utilizing flash back and flash forward, manipulation of focus and partially obscured vision, framing devices, montage, and similar techniques. The cinema's handling of eccentric point of view, delayed decoding, double exposure, and "trick" shots, seems to have analogues in "Heart of Darkness," *The Good Soldier*, and *Wide Sargasso Sea*. If Ford and Conrad really were consciously exploiting these techniques in texts written in 1898, they were trying to create cinema before the invention of much of the modern machinery used to create the illusion of moving pictures.

Conrad's *The Secret Agent* (1908) has as its central affair a botched attempt to bomb Greenwich Observatory. It is possible to view this work as an indirect discussion of the nature of time in fiction. Greenwich Observatory sets the universal standard for measurement of geographic space and time. Its mechanisms, even today, measure in microseconds the time used for navigational calculations throughout the world. As a ship's officer, Conrad must have observed the great globe at the observatory whose fall marked noon precisely so that ships on the Thames could synchronize their navigational chronometers visually.

In *The Secret Agent* a foreign embassy drives Mr. Verloc, assisted by the half-witted brother of his wife, Winnie, to attempt a bomb attack on the symbol of order and rational measurement at Greenwich. The attack fails when the boy, carrying the bomb, clumsily blows himself up.

As the Greenwich Observatory stands at the center of this affair, declaring that space and time are permanent, unchanging, univocal, measurable, the story teller renders his tale in remarkably fluid, cinematic time. A memorable example occurs when Verloc returns home after the fiasco has killed his wife's beloved brother. At the conclusion of Chapter 11, exhausted Verloc reclines on his couch and with rising erotic interest summons his grief-stricken wife to him. The wife, Winnie, is sickened at the though of touching this man who has caused the horrible death of her brother, Stevie. When Verloc calls her to "Come here," she picks up a kitchen knife and approaches him. The narrative then enters the mind of Verloc.

We see things distorted by fear and surprise, as Verloc saw them in his last few seconds alive:

> Mr. Verloc . . . was lying on his back and staring upwards. He saw partly on the ceiling and partly on the wall the moving shadow of an arm with a clenched hand holding a carving knife. It flickered up and down. Its movements were leisurely. They were leisurely enough for Mr. Verloc to recognize the limb and the weapon. They were leisurely enough for him to take in the full meaning of the portent, and to taste the flavour of death rising in his gorge. His wife had gone raving mad—murdering mad. They were leisurely enough for the first paralysing effect of this discovery to pass away before a resolute determination to come out victorious from the ghastly struggle with that armed lunatic. They were leisurely enough for Mr. Verloc to elaborate a plan of defence involving a dash behind the table, and the felling of the woman to the ground with a heavy wooden chair. But they were not leisurely enough to allow Mr. Verloc the time to move hand or foot. The knife was already planted in his breast. (573.05-27)

In narrating this scene, the story teller goes into slow motion, marked by repetition of the phrase, "They were leisurely enough," like the ticking of a clock, so contrasting the racing panic of Verloc's mind with the standard pace of life.

The slow motion of Verloc's death underlines the conjectures of Inspector Heat, the police officer who examines the shredded remains and body parts of Stevie after the mentally retarded boy has accidentally detonated the bomb while carrying it. Inspector Heat thinks that Stevie's death must have been instantaneous; but, then,

> No physiologist, and still less of a metaphysician, Chief Inspector Heat rose by the force of sympathy, which is a form of fear, above the vulgar conception of time. Instantaneous! He remembered all he had read in popular publications of long and terrifying dreams dreamed in the instant of waking; of the whole past life lived with frightful intensity by a drowning man as his doomed head bobs . . . Chief Inspector Heat . . . evolved a horrible notion that ages of atrocious pain and mental torture could be contained between two successive winks of an eye. (123.07-27)

Duration of time and cinematic fluidity of time appear to be a major, although undenominated, topic of *The Secret Agent*.

Inspector Heat's notion of temporal relativity is reinforced in the set-up or frame of the explosion. The bomb itself, of course, must have a fuse. The Professor who supplies the materials and design for the bomb is very proud that no London policeman will ever arrest him, because he always carries on his body an explosive charge attached to a rubber ball in his pocket. If a policeman threatens him, he has only to compress the ball and everyone in the vicinity will be blown to pieces. One of the awe struck conspirators observes that the explosion must be "instantaneous," but the Professor ruefully admits that unfortunately this is the only weakness of his plan. Some twenty seconds must elapse between pressing the rubber ball and the explosion.

When the other conspirators pause to consider the mental effort required to get through those twenty seconds, the Professor observes that finally all systems of defense depend on "force of personality." He calmly says,

> I have the means to make myself deadly, but that by itself, you understand, is absolutely nothing in the way of protection. What is effective is the belief those people have in my will to use the means. That's their *impression*. It is absolute. Therefore I am deadly. (95.01-07, emphasis added)

The ability to create an impression is the Professor's transcendent power.

The contrast between uniform time as measured by Greenwich Observatory and variable duration as experienced by individuals in *The Secret Agent* has its parallel in the cinema, as the uniform, one-way time by which the audience enters and leaves the movie theater does not match at all the greatly condensed fictive temporal structures represented there on the screen with the capacity for slow motion, repetition, fast forward, reverse action, flashback, stop action, and so on. The cinematic fluidity of fictional time contrasted to the apparent rigid uniformity of local clock time enters any story narrated by a persona. In "Heart of Darkness" for example, the outer time of the framing situation is marked by the turning of the tide as Marlow and his audience on the deck of the Nellie pass some six hours telling tales. Meanwhile the Congo adventures, which once occupied many months, are compressed and distorted through Marlow's telling, so as to fit into that six-hour frame.

Conrad and Ford were aware of philosophical problems posed by contrasting time schemes in fiction. Their collaboration on *The Inheritors* (1901) produced an aesthetically inferior work which, nevertheless, sheds light on their concern with the problem of fictional time. The central affair in *The Inheritors* is the attempt to exploit Greenland by building a railway and opening the country to European trade by the *Système Groenlandais*. The general situation in the plot of *The Inheritors* is transparently identical to that in the Congo valley where "Heart of Darkness" takes place: European capitalists hope to exploit a defenseless native population by building a railroad and reaping rapid profits from unscrupulous trade.

In *The Inheritors* the Duc de Mersch, the European advocate for the Trans-Greenland Railway, sounds remarkably like the Belgian propagandists supporting the opening of a rail link for Africa in Conrad's "Heart of Darkness." The Duc de Mersch says:

> [The railway's] importance to British trade was indisputable . . . It was the obvious duty of the British Government to give the financial guarantee. He would not insist upon the moral aspect of the work—it was unnecessary. Progress, improvement, civilization, a little less evil in the world—more light! It was our duty not to count the cost of humanising a lower race. Besides the thing would pay like another Suez canal. (81.05-13)

The text of *The Inheritors* traces the conflicting attitudes of various characters toward this scheme and the effect it has on their lives.

Like "Heart of Darkness," *The Inheritors* examines the unfortunate impact of European capitalism on primitive people. The *Système Groenlandais* turns out to be "neither more nor less than a corporate exploitation of unhappy Esquimaux" (80.28-29). The natives of Greenland are caught in an immense disaster mysteriously visited on them from afar, like the dying Africans in the grove of death at the first station in "Heart of Darkness." But whereas the African catastrophe really existed and is historically recorded in Conrad's eyewitness Congo Diary, the Greenland adventure exists merely in a fanciful, hypothetical heteratopia. Imperialist exploitation of the Congo is a deadly serious topic, perhaps so serious that Conrad and Ford were looking for some disguise to neutralize its political force, to shelter themselves from harsh retaliation by readers who did not want to see imperialism exposed. Today's readers, however, find a change of setting from the Congo to Greenland inept as anti-imperialist argumentation. Removing the political issue from Africa to Greenland trivializes it and renders it slightly comic.

Like "Heart of Darkness" *The Inheritors* provides an array of differing attitudes toward the colonial enterprise. The central character, Etchingham Granger, has a professional obligation as a newspaper reporter to get to the bottom of things and report what he sees, rather like Conrad himself writing his Congo journal of his impressions as an apprentice river pilot in Africa. Granger comes to see that the *Système Groenlandais* is merely cynical exploitation of the natives. Unfortunately, he is surrounded by social and economic forces which discourage him from publishing his opinion and which encourage him to join the conspiracy of silence and to participate in the big lie.

Granger's family is connected to the Prime Minister, Churchill, who is committed to support the Duc de Mersch. Moreover, Granger has worked with Churchill on a biography of Cromwell. Granger sincerely respects Churchill's virtues. It appears that Churchill is the dupe of the Duc de Mersch, rather than a knowing party to the crimes in Greenland. If Granger openly exposes the *Système Groenlandais*, he will destroy his family ties, damage his future, and betray Churchill, a man of real virtues whose motives Granger respects. Like "Heart of Darkness" *The Inheritors* explores the question: What sort of hero, under what conditions, will try to tell the truth about Europe's impact on primitive people? *The Inheritors* addresses the question: Why does a Marlow or a Granger lie?

In writing *The Inheritors* Conrad and Ford turn away from the political or moral dilemma of imperialism to foreground a love story between Granger and a strange young woman from the "fourth dimension." Such a choice, like the displacement of the imperial theme from Africa to Greenland, seems to be an artistic flaw. The story of Granger's courtship appears very commonplace, except for the characterization of his otherworldly beloved. She apparently arrives from outer space, announces that she inhabits the "fourth dimension" and that her race will soon take over the earth. She has the power to distort Granger's senses. Granger's desperate erotic longing for her affection and approval is never adequately motivated or explained. Throughout most of the novel, she successfully poses as his sister, fooling his relatives and friends. Finally, she rejects Granger's love, even after he has ruined himself to help her thwart the *Système Groenlandais*. Is this girl from the fourth dimension yet another example of Conrad's general inability to portray complex female characters?

Granger's final interview with her recalls Marlow's interview with Kurtz's Intended Bride. Granger has permitted the publication of information which will discredit the *Système Groenlandais*. He says:

> I wanted to see her, to finish it one way or another, and, at my aunt's house,
> I found her standing in an immense white room; waiting for me. There was
> a profusion of light. It left her absolutely shadowless, like a white statue in a
> gallery; inscrutable. (206.01-07)

Like Marlow before Kurtz's Intended, Granger finds that his words fail, "'I want
my . . . ' I could not think of the right word. It was either a reward or a just
due" (206.15-17). The girl's reply is harsh and unexpected:

> "You have done nothing at all," she said, "Nothing."
> "And yet," I said, "I was at the heart of it all."
> "Nothing at all," she repeated. "You were at the heart, yes; but at the heart of
> a machine." Her words carried a sort of strong conviction. I seemed suddenly
> to see an immense machine—unconcerned, soulless, but all its parts made up
> of bodies of men: a great mill grinding out the dust of centuries; a great
> wine-press. She was continuing her speech.
> "As for you—you are only a detail, like all the others; you are set in place
> because you would act as you did. It was in your character. We inherit the
> earth and you, your day is over." (206.21-207.03)

Granger's coy mistress is a very strange literary characterization, reminiscent
perhaps of the science fantasy of H. G. Wells. She says she comes from the
"fourth dimension." She has the ability to alter Granger's perceptions. Shortly
after he first meets her, she plays a trick with his vision as he looks at a church
tower: "The tower reeled out of perpendicular. One saw beyond it, not roofs, or
smoke, or hills, but an unrealized, an unrealizable infinity of space" (8.03-05).
The girl tells him that his vision is so distorted because he shares with her the
"rudiments of a sense" of the fourth dimension from which she comes.

The extensive emphasis in the opening pages of *The Inheritors* on the
"fourth dimension" (for example, see pages 9 to 11 of *The Inheritors* ) can
be explained in part as a reference to the ideas of Henri Bergson (1859-1941)
whose *Time and Free Will* (*Essai sur les données immédiates de la conscience*,
1889) has an elaborate theory of a "fourth dimension" at its core. Briefly
stated, Bergson's general argument is that many philosophic paradoxes result
from bogus quantification of states of consciousness. For example, there is
the paradox of a pendulum's motion: If it takes a pendulum one second to
complete an oscillation from point A to point B and to return to point A, at one
half second the pendulum will be stationary at B, at one quarter second it will
stationary midway between A and B. At any given fraction of time, it seems
that the pendulum will be stationary, occupying a single given point in its path.
No matter how small the fraction of time, the pendulum appears to be always
stationary at any given moment. How, then, does the pendulum get from one
stationary position to the next? How can motion exist at all?

Bergson maintains that the paradox of the pendulum's motion results from a failure to grasp the true nature of human perception.

> When I follow with my eyes on the dial of a clock the movement of the hand which corresponds to the oscillations of the pendulum, I do not measure duration, as seems to be thought; I merely count simultaneities, which is very different. Outside me, in space, there is never more than a single position of the hand and the pendulum, for nothing is left of the past positions. *Within myself a process of organization or interpenetration of conscious states is going on, which constitutes true duration.* It is because I *endure* in this way that I picture to myself what I call the past oscillations of the pendulum at the same time as I perceive the present oscillation. Now, let us withdraw for a moment the ego which thinks these so-called successive oscillations: there will never be more than a single oscillation, and indeed only a single position of the pendulum, and hence no duration. Withdraw, on the other hand, the pendulum and its oscillations; there will no longer be anything but the heterogeneous duration of the ego, without moments external to one another, without relation to number. Thus, within our ego, there is succession without mutual externality; outside the ego, in pure space, mutual externality without succession: mutual externality, since the present oscillation is radically distinct from the previous oscillation, which no longer exists; but no succession, since succession exists solely for the conscious spectator who keeps the past in mind and sets the two oscillations or their symbols side by side in auxiliary space.(*Time and Free Will*, translated by F. L. Pogson, 107-09)

The rational process of thought in the observing ego holds events in a sequence as if one event followed another. This juxtaposition of events in a sequence creates what Bergson calls "duration." The mental process is stimulated by static frames of observation. Through "duration" an observer creates both motion and causality. Motion is possible, or one thing seems to cause another, only because the mind persists in preserving the memory of events and disposing those events in a linear sequence as if they extended in space. Bergson's notion of static instants which are set in a moving, causal sequence by the observer's mind suggests a cinematic analogue: the impression on the retina of each viewer's eye of motion, causation, or general artistic design in the cinema is generated from a series of still frames observed in sequence.

William Faulkner (1897-1962) in the concluding words of *The Sound and the Fury* (1929), "They endured," casts the black servant Dilsey as a Bergsonian heroine. Her ego perceives the scattered events whose "sound and fury" would signify nothing without the duration of her mind. The observing ego in Faulkner's Dilsey, Conrad's Marlow, Ford's Dowell, or Rhys's Antoinette demonstrates Bergson's mental duration mounted on the chaos of immediate sensory data. These observers "endure" in the sense of Bergson: they provide a mental space, called by Bergson the "fourth dimension," in which static frames of sensory data are juxtaposed, related, and rendered meaningful.

"Heart of Darkness" and *The Inheritors* go over much of the same ground, but "Heart of Darkness" has superior artistic power because Conrad moves the issue of imperialism squarely into Africa where it actually takes place. He moves the theme of erotic love off stage in "Heart of Darkness" so as to concentrate on the political affair and the moral crisis in the story. Finally, he invents the character of Marlow to act out the process of duration. Marlow dramatizes the process of Bergsonian *duration* instead of talking indirectly about Bergson's ideas by reference to Granger's beloved prankster girl from the so-called "fourth dimension." Marlow's impressionist limited narration displays the vital moment, subsuming past and present, cause and effect, in Bergsonian pure duration.

# CHAPTER III
## EMPIRICAL BASIS OF IMPRESSIONISM

*Roots of Literary Impressionism: in the Impressionist Philosophy of David Hume; in Sensory Impressions as Data for Positivist Sociology in Auguste Comte; in French Impressionist Painting; in Henri Bergson's Vitalism and Pure Duration. The Authentic Experience.*

In *The March of Literature from Confucius to Modern Times* Ford celebrates the revival in Paris following World War I of the tradition he calls literary "impressionism":

> So the Divine Fire . . . the Flaubert-Maupassant-Rimbaud-Mallarmé-James-Conrad-impressionist fire—-burst out, once more in Paris . . . under the aegis of Mr. Pound . . . About him grouped themselves with a quite considerable adhesiveness, Mr. Joyce, Miss Stein, Mr. Ernest Hemingway, Mr. Glenway Westcott, Mr. E. E. Cummings and a whole Middle Western American group, as a rule from the University of Chicago . . . (ML 755-56)

When Ford denominates the word "impressionism," the roots of his concept reach backward in cultural history to several extra-literary sources. First, *impressionism* is commonly used to designate the theory of knowledge of David Hume and the British empirical philosophers. Second, it refers to the documentary recording of raw impressions and observations as a basis for "scientific" generalizations, in the manner of Auguste Comte or of scientific observers like Charles Darwin (1809-1882) in his record of the voyage of the *Beagle*. Third, it means French impressionist painting by Edouard Manet (1832-1883), Paul Cezanne (1839-1906), Claude Monet (1840-1926), Pierre Auguste Renoir (1841-1919), Paul Gauguin (1848-1903), Vincent Van Gogh (1853-90), Georges Seurat (1859-91), and their associates. Fourth, Ford's idea of impressionism coincides with the vital moment of authentic pure duration in the philosophy of Henri Bergson. For Ford, empirical philosophy, positive sociology, Bergsonian duration, and the revolution in French painting in the later Nineteenth Century combine to usher in the new age of literary impressionism.

According to Ford, literary impressionism was first cultivated as a movement in English writing when Ford and Conrad collaborated shortly before the turn of the century, but the movement flourished a second time on the Left Bank of Paris following the Great War, especially in the writers grouped around Ford's *Transatlantic Review*. When Jean Rhys met Ford in Paris, she stepped into a flourishing impressionist garden, complete with weeds and noxious plants mingled among the prize blossoms.

Ford attempts to explain how such diverse cultural strands are united in fiction written in the manner of Flaubert, James, or Conrad. In *Joseph Conrad: A Personal Remembrance*, Ford claims that he and Conrad "accepted without much protest the stigma 'impressionists' . . . because . . . we saw that life did not narrate, but made impressions on our brains. We in turn, if we wished to produce on you the effect of life, must not narrate but render impressions" (182). In this passage Ford's notions parallel David Hume's assertion in *A Treatise of Human Nature*, at the outset of "Book I: Of the Understanding":

> All the perceptions of the human mind resolve themselves into two distinct kinds, which I shall call *impressions* and *ideas*. The difference betwixt these consists in the degree of force and liveliness, with which they strike upon the mind, and make their way into our thought or consciousness. Those perceptions which enter with the most force and violence, we may name *impressions*; and, under this name, I comprehend all our sensations, passions, and emotions, as they make their first appearance in the soul. (15)

Ford, like Hume, gives priority to sensory perceptions in the formation of human understanding. In fiction, Ford assumes that the narrative voice or center of consciousness in a story is anthropomorphic, that the language constituting the fictional text is like a record or trace of thought in a particular human mind.

For Hume, the *impressions*, which come directly to the mind through the senses, have a greater vividness than *ideas*, which are merely faint memories of direct sensory impressions. Ideas can be for Hume either simple or complex. A simple idea is the memory of an actual sensory impression. So the mind receives an impression of a horse and remembers the idea of a horse afterwards. Complex ideas are structures built out of the association of such remembered simple ideas. Thus the complex idea of a centaur is constructed by the association of the simple idea of a horse with the simple idea of a man. Through a process of association of ideas, all our complex notions develop from simple ideas which are derived from sense impressions.

The effect of Hume's argument is to give precedence to sensory impressions in our mental life. Impressions are immediate and self-validating, whereas analytic thought follows from and is dependent on previous impressions and, of course, may be false or incorrect. Such a line of thought corresponds to the development of the dramatic monologue in poetry and the use of limited narration in fiction in its early stages. When the author attempts through a dramatic situation to foreground the immediate impressions of a character, giving priority to the way things seem to a particular mind in the act of encountering its environment, the text gains immediacy and validity. For example, Jonathan Swift's (1667-1745) invention of Lemuel Gulliver as reporter of his travels lends an air of credibility to his fantastic *Gulliver's Travels* (1726) much as Charles Darwin's (1809-82) personality lends firsthand authority to his strange report of *The Voyage of the Beagle* (1839).

Hume's psychology is also basic to the methods of the positivist scientists, who think that knowledge of the laws governing phenomena can only be discovered through careful and extensive observation of the phenomenal world so as to discover the logical principles posited in it. In this way, Auguste Comte proposes that the ultimate goal of positive sociology is to represent all social phenomena by a single generalization, in the way the "law" of gravity "explains" a very large range of physical phenomena. All real knowledge must be based on observed facts, which are nothing more than direct sensory impressions. It was in this sense that Emile Zola subtitled his Rougon-Macquart novels a "Biological and sociological history of a family under the Second Empire" ("Histoire naturelle and sociale d'une famille sous le Second Empire"). Zola, as a follower of Comte, believed that life is nothing more than the interaction of a biological organism with its environment. The novel is an imaginative projection of the way a particular biological organism registers its physical surroundings and responds to external stimuli. Zola's program for his novels is to record and document the raw impressions of life under the Second Empire so as to provide material for scientifically positive generalizations about human behavior.

In the same way, Arnold Bennett, gathering material for *The Old Wives' Tale*, records in *The Journals of Arnold Bennett*, in the entry for September 13, 1907:

> I bought Taine's *Voyage en Italie*, and was once again fired to make fuller notes of the *impressions* of the moment, of *choses vues*. Several good books by him consist of nothing else, I must surely by this time be a trained philosophic observer—fairly exact, and controlled by scientific principles. At the time one can scarcely judge what may be valuable later on. At the present moment I wish for instance, that some school mistress had written down simply her *impressions* of her years of training; I want them for my novel. The whole of life ought to be covered thus by *impressionists*, and a vast mass of new material of facts and sensations collected for use by historians, sociologists and novelists. I really must try to do my share of it more completely than I do. (254)

Bennett as well as Zola, Maupassant, or Flaubert intended to be a "realist" by recording impressions of the outer world as they impinge on a particular mind. The novel, then, is a union of invention and observation, an artistic statement of general ideas (of heredity, or history, or psychology, for example) based on a collection of *impressions* or observations of phenomena. The invented generalization is problematic and subject to verification. The impressions or observations are more certain, more fundamental, more real.

The realist writers like Zola or Bennett are positivists in the tradition of Comte. They study sensory impressions in order to discover the logic, the governing "law" or pattern, posited in human experience. As novelists search for the generalization or "law" of human behavior, however, their positive sociological goal breaks down. When impressions are presented in a work of fiction, the generalizations based on such impressions can never claim to be more than fictional, never claim to be certainly true for real human experience. The realist cannot establish the authority of scientific objectivity for his fictional observations. What strategy can the author employ to claim the authority of positive sociology for mere fiction?

The rise of literary impressionism at the turn of this century is a response to the disintegration of the project of naive realism. Ford's 1924 memoir of Conrad is an example of the impressionist's gambit. Although Conrad was a real person, any statement *about* Conrad will be unreal, incomplete, problematic, and subject to the charge of "untruth" or "distortion." A statement *about* experience is not the same as the experience itself. Ford, therefore, gives up any claim to the authority of realism in his memoir. It is apparently impossible to capture reality in a stream of words, which is a statement *about* experience, not the real thing. He does claim, however, that his text is true to his *impression* of Conrad and denies that any other impression has more authority than his own. We as readers are outraged at this posture, caught as we are in the convention that there must be a normative truth, that some impressions are better than others, that statements about experience must be treated as if they were real. Ford is taking a daring step in his "Preface" to his memoir of Conrad when he denies the normative center of truth lending authority to individual impressions.

Hume himself saw that to base all knowledge solely on sensory impressions made it impossible to prove a correspondence between the impressions perceived and the world exterior to the perceiving mind. Hume's impressionism creates the solipsist universe of modernism. Each individual becomes trapped in his or her separate, unique nervous system, unable to communicate with others. Such solipsism grows, side by side, from positivist sociology along with realistic fiction. The positivist begins by separating the perception of phenomena from the phenomena themselves, separating our impression of the world from the world itself. The impressionist ends by locking us into our private mental prison houses, unable to see the world beyond our individual impressions.

Since there is no sure correspondence between mental impressions and the exterior world stimulating those sensations, there can be no proof that the impressions in one mind are the same as those of any other mind when faced with the identical stimulus. Indeed, the assumption must be to the contrary, that no two minds ever form quite the same impressions. Walter Pater in the "Conclusion" to *The Renaissance* articulates this modernist anxiety, that no matter how solid experience seems to be when we register our sensations of external objects:

> When reflexion begins to act upon those objects they are dissipated under its influence; the cohesive force seems suspended like a trick of magic; each object is loosed into a group of impressions—color, odor, texture—in the mind of the observer. And if we continue to dwell in thought on this world, not of objects in the solidity with which language invests them, but of impressions, unstable, flickering, inconsistent, which burn and are extinguished with our consciousness of them, it contracts still further: the whole scope of observation is dwarfed to the narrow chamber of the individual mind. (234-35)

Not only does the experience of reality dissolve into impressions, but no two impressions can be alike, shaped as they are by distinctly different minds.

As Pater observes, "Experience, already reduced to a group of impressions, is ringed round for each of one of us by that thick wall of personality through which no real voice has ever pierced on its way to us, or from us to that which we can only conjecture to be without. Every one of those impressions is the impression of the individual in his isolation, each mind keeping as a solitary prisoner its own dream of a world" (*The Renaissance*, 235).

The impression in the perceiving mind is not the same as the stimulus which generates that impression. For example, Hermann Ludwig Ferdinand von Helmholtz (1821-1894), whose lectures "On the Relations of Optics to Painting" supply a scientific rationale for many of the techniques of French Impressionist painting (especially in Seurat), recurs to this separation of impression from external "reality" over and over again in his scientific demonstrations. In his essay "Harmony in Music" (1873), he describes the production of "Sound" by the siren, a device made of a circular sheet of metal with holes pierced around its circumference so that a stream of air can be directed against the holes while the metal sheet rotates. In this way vibrations are set up in the air as the stream of air is interrupted by the spinning metal surface and bursts of air are regularly permitted to flow through the passing holes.

At a certain speed of the siren's wheel's rotation, a piercing sound occurs. At a slower speed or at a higher speed of rotation, there is no sound audible even though there are vibrations set up in the surrounding air just as in the range audible to the human ear. Helmholtz explains this phenomenon as follows:

> When the siren is turned slowly, and hence the puffs of air succeed each other slowly, you hear no musical sound. By continually increasing rapidity of its revolution, no essential change is produced in the kind of vibration of the air. Nothing new happens externally to the ear. The only new result is the sensation experienced by the ear, which then for the first time begins to be affected by the agitation of the air. Hence the more rapid vibrations receive a new name, and are called Sound. If you admire paradoxes, you may say that aerial vibrations do not become sound until they fall upon a hearing ear." (*Popular Scientific Lectures*, 29, translated by A. J. Ellis).

Helmholtz apparently proves "scientifically" that the sensation or impression of sound is quite different from what is "really" there, the vibrations of air which stimulate the impression. How does the ear take an impression from the wave propagated in air?

> Now what does the ear do? . . . We must distinguish two different points—the audible *sensation*, as it is developed without any intellectual interference, and the *conception*, which we form in consequence of that sensation. We have, as it were, to distinguish between the material ear of the body and the spiritual ear of the mind. (*Popular Scientific Lectures*, 44, translated by A. J. Ellis)

Such a separation of impression from "reality" stresses the unknowability of the world external to our minds in all the studies of perception by Helmholtz, especially in the essay "On the Relation of Optics to Painting" so influential for Seurat. For Helmholtz the object of the artist is to evoke the impression, not necessarily to imitate the stimulus. For that reason, artists should study the impression as it impinges on the perceiving intellect. Helmholtz begins "On the Relation of Optics to Painting" with a comparison of the way sight and hearing process sensory impressions:

> The physiological study of the manner in which the perceptions of our senses originate, how impressions from without pass into our nerves, and how the condition of the latter is thereby altered, presents many points of contact with the theory of the fine arts. On a former occasion I endeavoured to establish such a relation between the physiology of the sense of hearing, and the theory of music. (*Popular Scientific Lectures*, 250-51, translated by E. Atkinson)

Helmholtz's ideas are key to the innovations in handling color by the scientific impressionist painter, Seurat. Seurat saw that it was possible to create an impression by a false or unnatural stimulus, a stimulus quite different from that which normally generates the desired impression. Seurat developed his pointillist technique so that dots of unmixed color stimulate an impression of shimmering tints nowhere actually present in the pigment on the canvas. Optical mixture occurs on the retina of the viewer's eye allowing the artist to create an illusion of greater luminosity than possible by mixing pigments before applying them to the painted surface. Such pointillist technique fulfills Helmholtz's prediction:

> The more immediate object of the painter is to produce in us by his palette a lively visual impression of the objects which he has endeavoured to represent. The aim, in a certain sense, is to produce a kind of optical illusion. (*Popular Scientific Lectures*, 251, translated by E. Atkinson)

Although impressions received through the senses are the only source of our knowledge of the world about us, these impressions do not correspond directly to that stimulating world external to the mind. The mind shapes and constructs the impression in its own mental terms. An unmediated experience of the exterior world is not possible. As Helmholtz apparently demonstrates, waves propagated in air are sometimes apprehended as giving the impression of sound, sometimes not. Even in the hard sciences, the ostensibly *objective* study of the phenomenal world is more properly seen as a study of the mind in the act of responding to stimulations coming to it from a world it can never directly encounter. There is no direct correspondence between the mental impression and whatever stimulates that impression exterior to the mind. An *objective* scientific record is properly seen as a set of *subjective* responses by a mind registering its impressions of data. In such contexts the meanings of the words *subjective* and *objective* in ordinary language become reversed.

"Authentic" experiencing of a thing requires that the self (in Greek "autos") actively enters into the act of forming its impression. Mechanical or inert response to stimulation destroys the feeling that we live in a vital world. How can the artist re-vitalize the inert data, make our experience authentic, metaphorically restore the waste land or cause the secret garden to bloom? What is the curse that blights the reader's experience of a text? The myth that a normative intention governs a text, often in the shape of its omniscient author, prescribes that there is a single, univocal, correct meaning in every text which all careful readers can discover, so closing their task of interpretation.

If the reader approaches fiction with the assumption that its meaning is univocal and predetermined, there is no possibility for engaged, authentic experiencing of the text. Often, in a classroom or discussion section in schools and universities, teachers observe the alarm and resentment in young readers if they are told that only one reading for a text is correct. When confronted by the convention of the normative meaning or of the author's intention, like a stern father patriarchally correcting an errant child, the young reader instinctively resists. The student may say something like, "But Satan is so very strong and attractive in *Paradise Lost*! You kill the work unless you allow the possibility of my reading of Satan as heroic." The student here feels the need for authentic interpretation of the text, for the involvement of each reader in the construction of the artifact, even when that personal interpretation contradicts an enormous weight of evidence in the story. No amount of historical evidence will heal the student's feeling of loss, if the teacher disallows the student's misprision. The issue is not whether Satan is heroic or villainous, but how the reader responds when authority is denied to each reader's personal interpretation. Does *authority* reside solely with the *author,* who creates the text, or with the *authentic* response of each reader?

Formal innovations in impressionist narrative are driven by a desire to restore authenticity to the reader's activity. The various forms of limited narration, such as the dramatic monologue in the poetry of Robert Browning and the complicated narrative framing devices in such works as Emily Brontë's *Wuthering Heights*, arise when the writer tries to show a mind shaping what it sees. Browning's monologues move beyond a concern merely to record raw data as directly as possible. For Browning each perceptive mind shapes its own experience in a way which is unique and ephemeral. In Browning's "My Last Duchess," for instance, the reader is more interested in the poem as a delineation of an eccentric and distorting point of view than as a clear reflection of the external world. To be sure, the poem is set in an Italian Renaissance art gallery in which a lifelike portrait of the Duke's late Duchess hangs curtained. To be sure, the scene takes place on the particular day in which the Duke negotiates the details of his coming wedding with an emissary of the new bride's family. No matter how detailed and vivid the time and place are imagined, there is no authentic interest for the reader of this text until the mind of the Duke begins to play there.

When the Duke, speaking as the persona in the dramatic monologue, mentally combines the external stimulation of this particular place and time with his dark past experiences, his attitudes and ideas color and shape everything. In turn, the reader now must resolve and judge the questions his speech opens. Only this Duke sees what his mind shapes as he looks at the portrait of his dead lady. Did he order her murder directly, or merely make her so unhappy that she died young? Does he feel any remorse, looking at the vivid portrait of his last duchess? At the conclusion of the poem, the statue of Neptune taming a sea horse which Klaus of Innsbruck cast, for example, has a significance peculiar to this Duke's mind, on this particular day, not generally present to any viewer under any other circumstances. It is left to the reader to judge whether the Duke breaks the will of the emissary and his wife as easily as Neptune manages his sea horse in this moment of domination.

The attempt to capture the ephemeral moment when the observing consciousness intersects with an external stimulus in an authentic experience sets French Impressionist painting apart from the mechanical, conventional, inert art of the official French salons in the Nineteenth century. The Impressionist revolution in art from the first Group Exhibition in 1874 in Paris until the eighth and final exhibition in 1886 occurs in a rich atmosphere of intellectual ferment. Direct contact between figures like Helmholtz and Seurat is well known, but there is a general sense in which the impressionist painters developed innovations in technique, structure, and style in response to a shifting notion of what constitutes reality and how art relates to reality.

In Conrad's "Heart of Darkness," in Ford's *The Good Soldier*, or in the passages in Ford's memoir *Joseph Conrad* constructing a sample of an impressionist narrative about a certain Mr. Slack, Ford finds characteristics in fiction which parallel scientific, or late impressionist painting, such as the works of Seurat or the paintings of Cezanne's later career. Impressionist novels are not narrations, mere reports of events. The sequence of events or plot in an impressionist novel is always reported by a story teller or dramatized persona. By limiting the narration to the words of a character, the author is suppressed from the pages of the book. In "Heart of Darkness" the tale is twice-told. The character Marlow tells the story one evening to a limited dramatic audience on board a ship in the Thames estuary and one of those present retells the tale to us. The story is like a stream of consciousness in that the memory and imagination of the inner speaker, Marlow, mingle with events occurring in the fictive present. The outer speaker's report of Marlow's tale, however, does not depict directly the flow of ideas across Marlow's mind. The stream of words and ideas has already been shaped into a story, into language, before it comes to the outer narrator's consciousness. The unnamed outer narrator, in turn, reshapes the story. Marlow gives us his impression of his experience in the Congo. The outer narrator gives us simultaneously his impression of Marlow's tale.

The main event or affair in "Heart of Darkness" has already happened, long ago. The dual time structure of the text sets up a fictive present scene as the story teller and his audience wait for the tide to turn on the Thames estuary, while Marlow's mind flashes back to remembered past events. We do not follow the sequence of events of the voyage up the Congo in the order in which they happened, but in digressive loops of association as the reader follows the story teller's mental process recounting the tale.

Frequently the reader's chronology of understanding is not in synchrony with the story teller's. For example, in "Heart of Darkness" the inner story teller, Marlow, speaks of his experience when he was piloting a Congo steamer through hostile jungle on his way up river to rescue the agent Kurtz:

> I was looking down at the sounding pole . . . when I saw my poleman give up the business suddenly, and stretch himself flat on the deck, without even taking the trouble to haul his pole in . . . At the same time the fireman, whom I could also see below me, sat down abruptly before his furnace and ducked his head. I was amazed. Then I had to look at the river mighty quick, because there was a snag in the fairway. Sticks, little sticks, were flying about—thick: they were whizzing before my nose, dropping below me, striking behind me against my pilot house. All this time the river, the shore, the woods were very quiet—perfectly quiet. I could only hear the heavy splashing thump of the stern-wheel and the patter of these things. We cleared the snag clumsily. Arrows, by Jove! We were being shot at . . . (109-110)

Ian Watt in *Conrad in the Nineteenth Century* (1979) calls such a lapse in time between the raw impression and the rational interpretation of that impression "delayed decoding" and considers it one of the chief characteristics of impressionist style.

In the "arrows by Jove" passage (above), the story teller takes us back to the remembered moment of his raw impression and recounts the sequence of events as they impinged on his senses at that time. He knows, when he is telling the tale, that the sticks were arrows. The reader probably guesses that they are arrows well before the story teller tells us so. The story teller, when he was acting out this scene in the Congo, was distracted by the snag and so could not give his full attention to analyzing the nature of the flying sticks at first, whereas the reader is free to focus his attention on the puzzle and arrive at the correct solution before the story teller. This divergence of understanding sets up a tension between the chronology in the reader's understanding and that of the more obtuse persona. We often encounter similar narrative structures in the detective story. The detective encounters some puzzling evidence and the reader, running ahead of the detective's mind, recognizes the key clue solving the mystery. The reader's understanding sometimes runs ahead of the narrator's, sometimes lags behind it, in the common detection plot, but the main interest of the reader lies in the comparison of the reader's understanding of things to the understanding of the detective.

The suppression of the author means the abdication of the role of all-knowing storyteller and its replacement by the psychological reaction of a character to the spectacle of the affair so that the raw impression, for example of flying sticks, precedes the more thoughtful explanation that they are arrows.

It is important to note that the first impression captured by Marlow, that there are little sticks flying through the air, is a false impression. When Ford uses the word *impression* in *The Good Soldier*, it frequently informs the reader that the previously stated impression is incorrect and subject to modification. Consider:

> I have given a wrong impression of Edward Ashburnham if I have made you think . . . (29.22);

> I trust I have not, in talking of his liabilities, given the impression that poor Edward was a promiscuous libertine. He was not . . . (64.11);

> I have given you a wrong impression if . . . (66.11);

> That was the impression I really had until just now . . . (99.11);

> When one discusses an affair——a long, sad affair——one goes back, one goes forward. One remembers points that one has forgotten and one explains them all the more minutely since one recognizes that one has forgotten to mention them in their proper places and that one may have given, by omitting them, a false impression. (209.15)

It is not necessary to cite here all twenty-five occurrences of the words *impression* and *impressions* in *The Good Soldier* to show that Ford customarily uses these words in a negated sense. Once something is recognized and named as an impression, it is already false and something new must take its place.

Impressions are strange *traces* of reality, lingering, inaccurate, demanding their updates. The process of telling a story has a stroboscopic effect, with each scene frozen momentarily, but fading out to be replaced by succeeding impressions. It is this sequence of falsehoods which constitutes the process of story telling. Caught in the stream of words signifying misunderstood ephemeral impressions, the authentic experience of the text becomes the ongoing process of reading. As each fleeting impression is erased by the subsequent impression, the text makes the reader a participant in the construction of the artifact by a process of constant updating.

There is a line in the rise of realism in fiction stretching from Emile Zola's *Le roman expérimental* (1880), back through Claude Bernard's *Introduction à l'étude de la médecine expérimental* (1865), to Auguste Comte's *Cours de philosophie positive* (1830-42). Comte championed what we call the scientific method, arguing that all real knowledge must come from careful and unbiased observation of the phenomenal world so as to find hidden there the logic posited in nature. The goal of the positivist is to capture all phenomena in one elegant law, as the law of inverse squares seems to cover a wide range of apparently diverse experience in physics and astronomy. For Comte, the sciences have gradually emerged in a sequence, beginning with astronomy, as each moves toward a positive or scientific basis. Only the extreme complexity of human behavior has so far prevented it, too, from yielding its secrets to scientific study. Comte subordinates the idea of man to that of external nature. For him, the laws of nature are simply "there" and man's duty is to discover them by careful observation and measurement. For Comte the mathematical model is at the core of knowledge.

Bernard takes up Comte's argument with regard to medicine, urging that we consider man a biological organism reacting to his environment. Therefore, human behavior is nothing more than the interaction of hereditary and environmental forces which can be measured and studied rationally. Bernard wishes to exclude the supernatural, witchcraft, religion, and the human soul, from the treatment of disease. For Bernard the symptoms of disease always stem from a physical, not a metaphysical cause.

Zola's theoretical study of fiction, *Le Roman experimental*, imitates Bernard's positivist study of medicine. Zola's series of the Rougon-Macquart novels displays his practical goal of studying a sociological situation, analyzing life under the French Second Empire as experienced by two branches of the same biological family tree. Zola demonstrates that the interaction of these genetic characters and the environment of the Second Empire in France produces corruption and disease. Zola is studying a diseased society by examining his characters' behaviors, where behavior is defined as the interaction of genetic heredity and physical environment. For Comte, Bernard, and Zola, reality is external and quantifiable, behavior can be studied like astronomy or physical science by finding the logic posited in observed data.

Henri Bergson in his preface to his *Essai sur les données immédiates de la conscience* (1889) argues, on the other hand, that all the traditional paradoxes of philosophy arise from carrying out in our use of language unwitting or surreptitious quantification of what cannot be reduced to numbers. Bergson observes that we necessarily express ourselves by means of words in discursive speech and that we usually construct ideas as if they were extended in space. Language itself causes us to establish between our ideas the same sharp discontinuity as between material objects. Such assimilation of things to thoughts is useful for everyday life and necessary in most of the sciences. In Bergson's view, however, all the traditional paradoxes of philosophy, such as the nature of physical motion or the problem of free will, arise from our tendency to place side by side in space occurrences which are not spatial, our illegitimate translation of the unextended into the extended, of quality into quantity, which occurs when we use language naively. Bergson asks such questions as, "How does it happen that we say that one feeling is greater than another?" *Greater* is a spatial metaphor generally meaning that A spatially contains B, when A is said to be greater than B. When we talk of one feeling as greater than another, we translate a non-spatial occurrence into a spatial relation. We spuriously translate quality into quantity and, he argues, such practice leads to paradoxes with no solution. One of the most important ideas in Bergson's work is his assertion that there is necessarily an incompatibility between the verbal statement *about* an experience and the nature of the experience itself.

If, as Bergson thinks, language deforms experience, how can the novelist capture states of mind in words without deforming them through bogus quantification? Bergson defines one of the main motives driving the impressionist writers to technical innovation in limited point of view, "unreliable narration," complex temporal structure, fragmented diction, and broken syntax. Instead of talking about a state of mind, simply naming some condition such as "confusion" or "alienation," how can the writer give the audience access directly, authentically, to the experience?

Dramatization can force the reader into a participatory role. For example, T. S. Eliot's "The Waste Land" has as a central concern the feeling of devastation and alienation widespread in modern culture. Rather than talking *about* feeling lost, disoriented, and threatened, T. S. Eliot constructs a verbal collage which makes the reader *feel* directly disorientation, confusion, and fear. Consider "The Burial of the Dead," the concluding paragraph of "Section 1" from T. S. Eliot's "The Waste Land," for example:

Unreal City,
Under the brown fog of a winter dawn,
A crowd flowed over London Bridge, so many,
I had not thought death had undone so many.
Sighs, short and infrequent, were exhaled,
And each man fixed his eyes before his feet.
Flowed up the hill and down King William Street,
To where Saint Mary Woolnoth kept the hours
With a dead sound on the final stroke of nine.
There I saw one I knew, and stopped him, crying: "Stetson!
"You who were with me in the ships at Mylae!
"That corpse you planted last year in your garden,
"Has it begun to sprout? Will it bloom this year?
"Or has the sudden frost disturbed its bed?
"Oh keep the Dog far hence, that's friend to men,
"Or with his nails he'll dig it up again!
"You! hypocrite lecteur!—mon semblable,—mon frére!"

These lines describe the dejected crowd early on a wintry day in London, but fade into a reference to Dante's observation in the *Inferno* that it is impossible to imagine so many people at once, all dead. The speaker then encounters someone named Stetson, refers to the battle at Mylae (260 B.C.) in the First Punic War, and, suggesting the pattern of the ritual death of ancient fertility deities, asks if the corpse buried in the garden has begun to sprout. Two lines follow paraphrasing or parodying John Webster's (d. 1625) play *The White Devil*. The passage concludes by quoting a line from Charles Baudelaire's *Fleurs du Mal*, "You! Hypocrite lecteur! - mon semblable - mon frère!" This collage of fragments of words from widely separated contexts does not talk *about* alienation and confusion; it *creates* the feeling of alienation and confusion in the reader. Students in the classroom desperately try to find the coherence in this passage, to tame it, to make it less threatening. The power of the collage, however, is to defy reduction to a statement about experience. It forces the reader to experience directly the impression of cultural dissolution, fearful disorientation, and alienation.

Although the idea of *literary impressionism* is gaining some acceptance as an explanation of the transition from Victorian to Modernist art, Ford's ideas have suffered much resistance. Perhaps most damaging to his position is the tendency to imagine that Ford's literary impressionism designates merely a vague parallel between the art of the novel at the end of the Victorian era and soft, romanticized, sentimental impressionist canvases like those painted by the early Renoir or Mary Cassatt (1845-1926). Literary impressionism does not resemble these soft-focus studies. When Ford writes about literary impressionism, he is evidently not thinking about such early impressionist painting. Ford's concern is with the nature of reality and how art connects with the phenomenal world.

From the exhibition of the *Salon des Refusés* in 1863 to the death of Seurat in 1891, there is a very vigorous movement in French painting, generally known as *impressionism*, a movement in rebellion against the academic art of its time. French impressionist painting can be divided into two phases. The earlier phase is sometimes called Romantic Impressionism. The later phase, called Scientific Impressionism, finds its center in the work of Seurat. It is this second phase, Scientific Impressionism, which most stimulates literary impressionism. The innovations in technique and structure in Scientific Impressionist art, like those in literary impressionism, are partly a response to the ideas of Comte and to the pressures brought to bear on Comte's position by Bergson.

Ford finds a rough parallel between French painting and fiction in the later Nineteenth Century. As he asserts in *The March of Literature from Confucius to Modern Times*:

> Art critics are accustomed to say that the history of the art of painting divides itself sharply in two parts. There was painting before Cezanne and there has been painting since Cezanne, but the objectives of the two modes of painting have scarcely any connection. A similar caesura is observable in the aesthetics of creative writing. There was writing before Flaubert; but Flaubert and his coterie opened, as it were, a window through which one saw the literary scene from an entirely new angle. (ML 731-2)

Impressionist painting in France develops in two waves. The earlier phase begins from realism and is concerned with treatment of low subjects in art, eccentric or private vision, and manipulation of point of view. This earlier movement is sometimes called romantic impressionism and is exemplified in the handling of limited point of view and framing angle in works by Degas such as *The Orchestra of the Paris Opera* (1868-9) or *L'Etoile* (1878), the eccentricity of vision in such works as Monet's *Impression Fog (Le Havre)* dated 1872, and Manet's low subjects in the infamous *Olympia* (1863) or *Le Déjeuner sur l'herbe* (1863). From the problems of point of view and eccentric perception posed by romantic impressionism springs a second wave of technical innovation among artists experimenting with light, form, and color. This second wave is sometimes called scientific impressionism, characterized by the techniques of pointillism and optical mixture of color developed by Seurat and Van Gogh, and by the abstraction of form and planes of vision found in the later work of Cezanne. It points toward the Fauve and Cubist movement.

Scientific impressionism exploits the constructive role of the viewer to an unusual degree. A key concept for the scientific impressionist is pointillism, which depends on the blending in the eye of each beholder dots on the canvas into colors and shapes nowhere explicitly depicted. Impressionism begins by trying to record the act of perception, to show how we register our perceptions of the exterior world; but it ends by trying to control the response of the audience to the stimulating artifact, to manipulate the constructive activity of the viewer.

At the outset impressionism in painting espouses the realism of artists like Courbet in revolt against allegorical classicism and romantic anecdotal subjects. By painting from life in the open air events from everyday life, the artist hopes to mirror reality. Such a desire for an accurate reflection soon leads to an examination of the reflecting surface. A single object is not the same when seen from differing points of view or under different conditions of light or fog, as illustrated by Monet's series of paintings of the same haystacks at different times of day or of the facade of Rouen Cathedral under various weather and lighting. Monet's attempts to capture the fleeting instantaneity of the image. The haystack at dawn disappears into the haystack at noon, neither image is permanent nor absolutely true. The perceiving mind and the conditions of perception conspire to construct an image which is immediately out of date as the changes of nature flow on.

How to capture this quality of elusive change? Monet's answer in *Boulevard des Capucines* (1873) is to paint a fairly detailed depiction of the street in which human figures are represented by quick dashes or splotches of dark pigment, perhaps slapped on the canvas by a quick jerk of the brush rather than carefully drawn. Monet is paradoxically trying for a super realism by introducing chance, randomness, and imprecision into his work. By introducing chance disposition of his subject matter he hopes to evade the charge of artificiality. By scattering the images of people along the street less formally than in an academic pose, he hopes to be even more true to the unplanned nature of real experience. Yet his attempt is self-defeating, for even as he abandons formal arrangement, he nevertheless exercises the creator's choice to select one figure over another, one structure over another, in treating his subject. Clearly, Monet gives only the impression of chance, not chance itself in the disposition of the figures strolling along the boulevard.

The unfinished nature of the detail, the roughness of the surface, and the incompleteness of the painting are attempts to capture the real limitations of an observer's impressions. If Monet does not paint a finished anatomical representation of each figure in his *Boulevard des Capucines*, the level of detail indicates the limited amount of information which might consciously be registered in a quick glance at the scene. If the chance observer would not notice it, Monet does not paint it in. The artist is not trying to represent the scene as it truly is, but as it would be perceived. This unfinished aspect of impressionist art was the source of much hilarity among the critics of the first impressionist show. Louis Leroy in "Exhibition of the Impressionists," in *Charivari*, April 25, 1874, imagines a dialogue between an academic painter and the critic viewing the show. The academic painter sees Monet's *Boulevard des Capucines* and asks what are the "black tongue lickings in the lower part of the canvas." When told that they represent people, he replies, "Is that the way I look when I am walking along the Boulevard des Capucines?" But the painting which drives him completely off balance is Monet's *Impression Sunrise*. "Wallpaper in its most embryonic state is more finished than that seascape," he cries, beginning a mad dance through the exhibition gallery.

Paintings like Monet's *Impression Sunrise* or *Impression Fog: Le Havre* are extremely crude canvases in which a few splashes and whirls of color represent the sun, its reflection, the shadow of a boat perhaps seen indistinctly through the fog. These pictures do not clearly mirror their ostensible subjects; but, rather, try to capture the act of imperfect perception under peculiarly difficult conditions, obscured by fog. This, too, is an attempt to introduce an aleatory, random, or chance element into the artifact and to shift from the naively realistic aim of depicting the world as it really is, to the way it really appears to a particular perceiving intelligence, on a particular day, under particular circumstances which in all likelihood can never be repeated.

We might consider Monet's *Impression Fog: Le Havre* as a visual monologue, like one of Robert Browning's dramatic monologues. In both cases, when the audience experiences the artifact, attention shifts from what is seen to how it is seen. The artifact does not mimic the phenomenal nor the ideal world, but attempts to capture the act of experiencing. To force his readers to recognize that his dramatic poems were representations of the act of experiencing by unique centers of consciousness, Browning hit upon the form of giving multiple versions of the same affair as experienced by an array of different characters, thus producing a series of conflicting versions from which the reader must derive his or her own view of the case.

In *The Ring and the Book*, Browning imposed ten different versions of the affair reported in *The Old Yellow Book* of the trial and execution of Count Guido Franceschini, confessed murderer of his child wife. The case actually occurred. The historical events are constant, but Browning relates them over and over through differing limited narrators: Count Guido himself, his wife Pompilia, the handsome priest Caponsacchi who may have been the wife's lover, the Pope, Half Rome, the Other Half Rome, and so on. This subtle and rich form forces the reader to see that Browning is delineating the act of experiencing in dissimilar minds. Each reader is compelled to judge and so construct the state of affairs as it appears to her or to him. The way Guido sees Pompilia's conduct and the way Caponsacchi sees the same phenomena are contradictory and the poem as a whole is about such differences in the nature and quality of human experience.

Browning's poetic form parallels Monet's practice of painting a series of canvases all showing the same haystacks or the same facade of Rouen Cathedral at different times of day and under differing weather conditions. These are all methods of forcing the audience to recognize that the phenomenal world is not constant, that each mind at each instant forms various impressions of the exterior world, and that the task of the artist is to represent these acts of experiencing. If Browning's dramatic monologues are sometimes called the poetry of experience, the impressionist haystacks of Monet might be called paintings of experience.

Ford maintains that Conrad and he wrote fiction in the same ideological context as the French scientific impressionist painters. When Ford identifies the painting of Cezanne as a watershed in western art, he is probably thinking of Cezanne's *Mont Sainte-Victoire* (1885-87), which was an obsession in Cezanne's artistic development. Mont Sainte-Victoire is a mountain near Aix where Cezanne spent his childhood. We can recognize the contour and general features of the real landscape in Cezanne's canvas, yet the painting is executed in geometric patches of blue, green, and earth tones. If we did not know its title, we probably would read it as abstract, not referring to a subject standing outside the canvas. The ominous and disturbing masses of color thrusting up out of the plane of the canvas suggest that this image expresses a peculiar disturbance in the particular mind of the observer. The sense that *Mont Sainte-Victoire* represents some weighty anxiety in the artist is reinforced by the fact that Cezanne found it a very difficult canvas to complete and put aside. We might suggest that the artist has sacrificed loco-descriptive realism in this case to emphasize psychological realism, obscuring the reflective image of a real geographical location so as to emphasize the spiritual state of the observer. As Ford says, this is the crucial circumstance in *Mont Sainte-Victoire* where "all you get are the spectacle of the affair and the psychological reaction " (ML 768) to it.

Although Ford defines the superimposition of a psychological reaction simultaneously onto the spectacle of an affair as the basic condition of impressionist art, Cezanne's painting does more. The structure of the picture is governed by three conflicting imperatives: It refers to a real locus in southern France. It projects an agitated state of mind and expresses a set of attitudes rooted in the point of view which shapes and frames the scene. But, also, it forces the viewer into a constructive activity by juxtaposing blocks of color, manipulating planes, and defamiliarizing the ostensible subject to such a degree that it is barely recognizable. If the artist's aims were realistic, the first of these imperatives would be dominant and he would try to make the scene look like a photograph of the terrain. If the second were dominant, he would be an expressionist, and feel free to compose his picture like a dream or nightmare; free to paint devils, monsters, boiling flames, and to violate all mimetic restraints. But the work is impressionist, barely acceptable as representation of the locus, yet capturing the activity of a mind perceiving that environment and, at the same time, forcing the viewer to participate in the act of perception.

Ford's *The March of Literature from Confucius to Modern Times* hinges on the shift which he believes occurs when the artist no longer tries to mirror the external world in its general or universal aspect and tries, instead, to capture the act of a particular intelligence in its unique and immediate experience.

When Ford uses the word *impressionism*, he is thinking of Hume's theory of knowledge, but more immediately he has in mind the later phase of French Impressionist painting, the phase following Cezanne, the scientific impressionism exemplified in the painting of the later Cezanne, Van Gogh, and Seurat, as opposed to the earlier romantic impressionism of Manet, Monet, or Degas.

Scientific impressionism in painting can be intuitive like Van Gogh's or developed systematically from a close study of experimental science as was Seurat's. In both cases the artist seeks to develop techniques in art which exploit the constructive response of the viewer more powerfully than previously possible. For example, Seurat's practice of pointillism and optical mixture of color came from his careful study of perception, color, and the propagation of light by Helmholtz, Michel-Eugene Chevreul's *De la loi du contraste simultané des couleurs*, Charles Blanc's *Grammaire des arts du dessin*, and Ogden N. Rood's *Modern Chromatics*. Simply stated, the basis of Seurat's theory of optical mixture of colors is that an impression of greater luminosity can be obtained by juxtaposing dots of unmixed primary colors so that they blend in the eye of the observer into the desired effect, rather than by trying to produce the color by mixing pigments and applying the mixture to the canvas. An effect of green produced by the fusion on the retina of the eye of juxtaposed separate dots of pure blue and pure yellow will be brighter than that obtained by mixing the pigments so as to put green on the canvas. Seurat's pointillist technique used carefully calculated dots of pigment to create an optical mixture, when viewed from the proper distance, to produce shimmering images constructed on the retina of the eye of each viewer but nowhere actually depicted on the physical canvas.

From Chevreul, Seurat further developed the theory that a work of art must be a harmony formed from the interconnected analogy of color, value, hue, and line. He constructed elaborate formal abstractions in the lines and shapes of his figures which were intended to reinforce the contrasts of color and blend into a multi-dimensional harmony when perceived by the spectator. Seurat demands such a highly constructive activity from the viewer because verisimilitude in art means to him that the activity of the spectator must imitate the activity of real perception. Seurat's use of juxtaposition, fragmentation, contrast, and defamiliarization have their counterparts in impressionist prose and poetry.

The physiological study of perception by scientists like Helmholtz shows how Hume's impressionist philosophy (basing all human knowledge on sensory impressions of an exterior world) and Comte's sociological positivism (positing a logic in all phenomena) lead to the shimmering haze of a pointillist canvas by Seurat and the verbal collages of Conrad and Ford. Helmholtz is not only an original investigator, but also a powerful popularizer of the specialized research going forward on many fronts in the science of the later Nineteenth Century. It is well-known, of course, that his study of light and color was one of Seurat's main ideological sources, but there is a wider aspect to his approach to the phenomenal world. Typically he separates the *impression* received by our senses from the external *stimulus* which generates that impression. Waves in air produce the impression of sound only when they fall within the auditory range, although the same sort of waves exist unheard at higher and lower frequencies. The impression of sound is, for Helmholtz, a perceptive activity. He often observes that the study of how external impressions impinge on the nervous system presents many points in common among the arts. Art is a kind of illusion, a condition in which unknowable stimuli evoke impressions which have no direct equivalents in the external world. In studies such as his "Recent Progress in the Theory of Vision" (1868), he stresses the constructive activity of the perceiving mind and he moves the locus of reality into the activity of perception. *Relations*, such as contrast, comparison, and surprising juxtaposition lie at the center of his visual demonstrations of physical perception, as they do for Seurat's theory of color and Ford's theory of the verbal collage.

# CHAPTER IV
## JEAN RHYS AND FORD: AN IMPRESSIONIST AFFAIR

*Jean Rhys and the development of literary impressionism. Open versus closed fiction. Turbulent recurrence of denominated concepts. Competing cognitive and affective frames. Leitmotif. Authentic engagement of reader and text.*

In 1924 Ford and Jean Rhys had their brief encounter. Ford's *Transatlantic Review* was failing, his memoir of Conrad triggered Jessie Conrad's bitter personal attack, and, chronically short of money, he was living precariously with Stella Bowen in Paris. He was also beginning his most ambitious work, the Tietjens Tetralogy. Rhys was penniless and out of work while her husband was in prison; but she stood at the beginning of a very talented, if painful, career as a writer. Her contact with Ford brought to her the tools to free her voice. Literary impressionism rendered her eloquent.

Rhys had grown up in the West Indies, daughter of a Creole mother and a Welsh doctor. In 1916 she went to England to study. The cold climate there nearly killed her, symbolically expressing the chilling alienation she felt as a technically "colored" colonial in the capital city. As an impoverished, but strikingly beautiful, young woman trying to earn a living as an actress and model, she was the very stereotype of virtue in danger, like some country girl come to town in a set of prints by William Hogarth (1697-1764). Eventually, she drifted into Ford's circle on the Left Bank in Paris after World War I—friendless and vulnerable. Ford and Stella invited her to live with them temporarily and Ford encouraged her to write fiction. When the relationship between Ford and Rhys became intimate, Stella and Ford soon dropped her.

What was merely another casual episode in Ford's generally untidy private life was something much more serious and painful for Rhys, as recorded in her *Postures* and *After Leaving Mr. Mackenzie*. Late in her life, there was some compensation for her early harsh treatment from Ford. Rhys eventually saw herself hailed in *The New York Times* as the greatest living novelist on the occasion of the publication of her *Wide Sargasso Sea* (1966). Such a claim could never have been made about Ford himself, except perhaps in an autobiographical vein. Yet, Rhys carries forward the tradition of Ford and Conrad. *Wide Sargasso Sea* best displays its virtues when it is placed in the sequence of impressionist masterpieces: Flaubert's *Madame Bovary*; Conrad's "Heart of Darkness" and *Lord Jim*; and Ford's *The Good Soldier* and the Tietjens Tetralogy. The appropriate position for Rhys is at the vanguard of the march of literary impressionism.

*Wide Sargasso Sea* originates in Charlotte Brontë's *Jane Eyre* (1847). Jane is prevented from marrying Rochester because he has hidden away a mad West

Indian wife, called Antoinette or Bertha, who finally perishes in the fire she sets, burning down Rochester's ancestral home and blinding him. Only after the conflagration can Jane and Rochester be united. It is easy to see that the author, Rhys, a poor alien, feeling betrayed by the English and apparently wealthy (or at least middle class) Stella Bowen and Ford, might find her personal anxieties embedded in Charlotte Brontë's work. Rhys easily might cast herself in the part of the alien West Indian woman wrongly deprived of her man's love.

The contemporary reader may smile at the idea of Ford playing the role of Rochester, but for Rhys it was no joke. In *Jane Eyre* the West Indian wife is seen entirely from the exterior, and she lurks as a fearsome, dark presence in Rochester's house. Seen mainly through the eyes of her English rival, she naturally takes on a hideousness altogether unbearable. In these words Rochester reveals her existence (in Chapter XVI):

> Bertha Mason is mad; and she came of a mad family;—idiots and maniacs through three generations! Her mother, the Creole, was both a mad woman and a drunkard!—as I found out after I had wed the daughter: for they were silent on family secrets before. Bertha, like a dutiful child, copied her parent in both points. (JE 597.09-16)

When Jane looks on the madwoman she sees:

> In the deep shade at the further end of the room, a figure ran backwards and forwards. What it was, whether beast or human being, one could not, at first sight, tell: it grovelled, seemingly, on all fours; it snatched and growled like some strange wild animal: but it was covered with clothing; and a quantity of dark, grizzled hair, wild as a mane, hid its head and face. (JE 599.13-21)

The "hyena" with "bloated features" attacks Rochester in this scene, biting his cheek before being subdued.

*Wide Sargasso Sea* is the sympathetic history of this madwoman from her youth in the West Indies until the moment when she takes her candle to fire Rochester's home. Much of the tale is told by stream of consciousness, looking through the eyes of Antoinette (alias Bertha). On the simplest level, we can imagine *Wide Sargasso Sea* as an attempt to render justice, to present the alien woman's point of view and plead her case, or to explain plausibly how she and her husband have got to the sorry state evident in *Jane Eyre*.

Part I of *Wide Sargasso Sea* is narrated by Antoinette, who was growing up in Jamaica shortly after the passage of the emancipation act of 1833 by the Imperial Parliament. Slaves were not actually freed until 1838 after a period of "apprenticeship." Nevertheless, among the European colonial elite there was great fear of violence from the newly freed blacks and expectation of economic ruin for the slave-powered sugar plantations. Because of her Creole background,

Antoinette is outcast from both the white and the black communities, in a state in which civil disorder and violent intimidation are common.

Isolated, fearful, impoverished, she lives at Coulibri, the crumbling estate of her widowed mother. Her closest companion is Christophine, a Martinique obeah woman, a voodoo witch. Her mother remarries to an Englishman, Mr. Mason, and their family fortunes improve temporarily until the black community hears that Mason intends to import Asian coolies to displace them on the plantation. The blacks revolt, burning Coulibri and killing her half-wit brother. In town, she goes to convent school, and a colored "cousin" Sandi protects her from more hostile blacks.

Part II of the tale shifts to young Rochester as narrator on the honeymoon trip of the couple into the mountains to Coulibri. Following the details of the fictive "reality" outlined by Charlotte Brontë, Rochester reveals how his marriage to Antoinette was arranged for financial reasons. After a period of uneasy passion, Rochester receives a denunciation of Antoinette from another half-caste colored "cousin," Daniel Cosway, who accuses her of incipient madness and unchaste behavior with Sandi. As Rochester's doubts grow, Antoinette procures a love potion from Christophine. True to its nature, the potion works for one night only. Antoinette, her future now entirely in Rochester's control and surrounded by hostility, is torn away from her native land, transported to England, to confinement, and to her final suicidal act.

Rhys saw that Charlotte Brontë's presentation of the evil madwoman and the completely dead love of Rochester demanded a more fully fleshed, more rounded treatment. After reading the text by Rhys, we "see round" Antoinette in a new way. Rhys evokes our sympathy for Antoinette and we become aware of the limitations of Brontë's Rochester. The evident shortcomings of Jane Eyre's future husband are strangely ignored in Charlotte Brontë's novel, glossed over silently. Bringing Rhys's text to bear on Charlotte Brontë's not only develops the blank character of Antoinette, but converts Rochester into a much more interesting, equivocal figure. Rhys rounds Charlotte Brontë's flat characters so that the reader questions Jane Eyre's judgment. "Why is Jane so uncritical of Rochester?" we ask as we turn from *Wide Sargasso Sea* to *Jane Eyre*.

It is not unusual for a novelist to base a story on another writer's fiction. George Macdonald Fraser's *Flashman* (1970) and its sequels, for instance, purports to follow the career of the villain of Thomas Hughes's *Tom Brown's Schooldays* (1856), showing that the nasty schoolboy, Flashman, is the veritable hero of Victorian Imperialism. T. H. White's charming *Mistress Masham's Repose* (1946) treats Swift's Lilliputians rediscovered by an English school girl as a paradigm for English colonial paternalism. Rhys similarly raises issues latent in Charlotte Brontë's text: the English fear and suspicion of foreigners and the evil of male economic and social domination. But Rhys goes further than Fraser or White. *Mistress Masham's Repose* does not alter our reading of *Gulliver's Travels* (1726); but once we have read *Wide Sargasso Sea*, we can never again read *Jane Eyre* in quite the same way. The power to reach into the past and *transform* the nature of a previous text is the mark of high critical power which *Wide Sargasso Sea* derives from literary impressionism as practiced by Ford and Conrad in their best work.

The affair at the center of *Wide Sargasso Sea* is Antoinette's insane, suicidal conflagration, an event which has already happened, like Jim's abandonment of the Patna in *Lord Jim*, the disintegration of the foursome in *The Good Soldier*, or the death of Kurtz in "Heart of Darkness." The story progresses in widening circles of understanding as the reader sees the scene through the eyes of one or more witnesses and tries to judge what the facts of the equivocal case may be. In such stories the reader struggles with multiple, limited, unreliable narrations in order to deduce and judge the true state of the affair. The plot is open to multiple, contradictory interpretations. Was Antoinette guilty of unchaste acts with Sandi? Or is she mad and only imagining such scenes? Is the voodoo love potion of Christophine really magic? Or is it, as Rochester thinks, merely poison? When Rochester confronts Christophine and says, "I would give my eyes never to have seen this abominable place," is Christophine "really" a witch when she replies, "And that's the first damn word of truth you speak" (161). Is all of *Jane Eyre* nothing but the working out of a voodoo curse? A curse pronounced in another book written over a century after the publication of *Jane Eyre*?

Since *Wide Sargasso Sea* is told in limited narration, it follows the psychological processes of the speakers—in Antoinette's case the mental processes of an alleged madwoman. What is fictive reality, what demented vision? The story shifts freely from reportage to fantasy. For example, at the end of *Wide Sargasso Sea*, the madwoman Antoinette describes, in detail which corresponds point for point with Charlotte Brontë's text, her setting fire to Rochester's house and perishing in the flames despite Rochester's efforts to save her. The reader has no reason to suspect that these paragraphs are not fictive reality until Antoinette says she "woke" to find her nurse, Grace Poole, watching her. She says, "I must have been dreaming" (190). But now she knows what she must do and within a few lines she takes up the candle to enact, presumably, the vision she has just dreamed. As in the fiction of Jorge Luis Borges or Robert Coover, the unwary reader is soon entangled in a confused web of shifting levels of reality in the text.

Moreover, *Wide Sargasso Sea* is told through multiple, limited narration. Charlotte Brontë's *Jane Eyre* gives us Jane's limited view of the affair. Rhys mounts onto that story the contradictory versions of the madwoman in the attic and that of Rochester. The reader, as usual in the impressionist narration of an affair, is forced into a constructive role, like a jury weighing and evaluating the truth of unreliable witnesses. But the very words, "unreliable narration," reveal the impressionist author's trickery. In a courtroom a witness is called "unreliable" when the report does not match the event, perhaps because the witness is biased, dishonest, or ignorant of the facts.

Fiction, however, is not like a real courtroom. There is no real event standing behind the report. Where a jury tries to penetrate an unreliable report and find the facts, the reader of fiction merely constructs a second, unstated fiction in place of the initial, unsatisfactory, stated fiction. An "unreliable" report in fiction is so stated that the reader constructs a second version of the affair. Such an unstated fiction is constructed by the reader to be more satisfactory than the fiction as stated by the text. This constructed second version of the affair is just as fictional as the unreliable first version. The two versions differ, not in their truth content, but in the conventions of the two stories. Perhaps the unreliable fiction as initially stated has internal contradictions or seems incomplete, with missing gaps and unexplained events. Perhaps it violates our customary ideas of time, space, causality, or identity. The second version constructed by the reader attempts to solve these problems, but it will be just as fictional as its less satisfactory unreliable version.

Some unreliable narrations can be solved. Mystery stories often tell the tale with a missing gap or apparent impossibility, until the reader (sometimes guided by the detective) retells the tale in an acceptable version. The text and the reader finally agree that the mystery has been solved, so achieving narrative closure. Many fictions, however, defy such simple closure and platoons of clever literary scholars feel compelled to construct their conflicting versions restating the initial narrative: Why does Hamlet hesitate to act? Are the ghosts in James's *Turn of the Screw* real or merely a figment of the deranged governess's imagination? Why does Marlow lie to the Intended Bride of Kurtz at the conclusion of Conrad's "Heart of Darkness"? Such questions remain open after many careful readings of the text.

Charlotte Brontë's *Jane Eyre* taken by itself is a closed narrative, ending in marriage, apparently with no unexplained gaps in the story. When *Wide Sargasso Sea* is juxtaposed with *Jane Eyre*, part of the "unearned increment," the increased significance of the two texts taken together, is that the affair is opened.

The second reading of a closed narrative lacks the interest of its first reading. A mediocre mystery or detective story is used up in a single reading. The reader discovers who done it and feels that a second reading would be useless. In this sense Charlotte Brontë's *Jane Eyre* appears to be closed. We know at the end of our first reading of the text who done it. The dark shape in Rochester's house is revealed and purged. Jane and Rochester are to live happily ever after. Contrast such a closed plot to the more open *Villette* by Charlotte Brontë, which draws the reader back a second time by leaving important questions unresolved.

With *Wide Sargasso Sea* Rhys opens *Jane Eyre*. It is this opening which alters the reader's relation to the text of Charlotte Brontë's novel and so seems to change the meaning of text. Even if *Wide Sargasso Sea* is a misreading, a mistake or misprision, it shifts the activity of the reader so that we are driven back to re-encounter Charlotte Brontë's version. Impressionist juxtaposition of Rhys's Antoinette and Charlotte Brontë's Jane Eyre destroys narrative closure, forces the reader to judge afresh Charlotte Brontë's opinions. *Wide Sargasso Sea* reaches into the past and seems to alter the meaning of the previous text.

The general situation of Rochester's alien, mistreated wife recurs frequently in Rhys's other works. For example, in *Good Morning, Midnight* one of Sasha Jansen's gentlemen friends tells her of an incident that happened when he was living in a room near Notting Hill Gate in London. Hearing an eerie cry in the passage outside his room, he finds a half-Negro woman lying weeping on the floor. She tells him she is from Martinique. She was living with an Englishman on the top floor of the house, but for two years had not gone out of her room except after dark. She finally ventures forth and meets a little English girl on the stairs who says that she is dirty, smells bad, and has no right to be in the house. The child says, "I hate you and I wish you were dead." The mulatto woman drinks a whole bottle of whisky and falls drunk in the hallway. After that there is only unbearable hatred toward her from the other women in the house.

Another example: in Rhys's short story, "Let Them Call It Jazz," the West Indian Selina lives at Notting Hill Gate until her money is stolen. Temporarily given shelter by a man in an ancient, decaying house, she lives in isolation, until through the hostility of her English neighbors she is sent to prison for disorderly conduct. While in Holloway prison, she hears a woman confined to the punishment cells, high in a turret, sing the "Holloway Song," letting her fellow prisoners know that she is equal to her ordeal. When Selina is released, she sings the song for a musician who turns it into a trivial jazz tune. In such stories, an alien, half-caste, West Indian woman is emotionally and financially dependent on an Englishman, who abandons her to the prejudice and hostility of English society. She is confined to a room high in a Gothic structure, misunderstood, drinks heavily, and is goaded to self-destructive activity.

Once we have defined a general pattern for works overtly similar to *Wide Sargasso Sea*, we can see that there is a widespread repetitive pattern in *all* the fiction by Rhys. She tells the same powerful feminist plea over and over. All her stories are about the indignity, the personal damage, which flows from a woman's financial and emotional dependence on men in an alien world. In a society in which she is systematically denied the right of self-sufficing employment, what can a woman do to maintain her freedom? Perhaps only symbolic gestures are possible. In *Good Morning, Midnight*, for example, Sasha Jansen refuses to sell herself and refuses to buy a gigolo. In the concluding scene, in order to avoid rape, she tells a man to take whatever money she has from her dresser drawer and to get out. When he has left, she finds he has not, in fact, taken all her money. As she lies alone in the darkness, in a collage mixing hallucination with fictive reality, she imagines him returning to her bed, and opens the door for him, only to receive the truly slimy man in a dressing gown who lurks in the hotel corridor. It is a bitter ending to a devastating story. Perhaps Rhys sees the area of female freedom so restricted that only such a choice is free from the taint of the marketplace in European society.

The main theme of her later fiction is stated in her first book, a collection of impressionist sketches, *The Left Bank* (1927). Ford wrote in the preface for this work that he wanted to be associated with Rhys because "hundreds of years hence" when "her ashes are translated to the Pantheon, in the voluminous pall . . . a grain or so of my scattered and forgotten dust may go in too, in the folds" ("Preface to Stories from *The Left Bank*" reprinted in Jean Rhys, *Tigers Are Better-Looking, with a selection from The Left Bank*, 150). Ironically, Ford's prophecy may turn out to be more nearly true than he expected in 1927.

In the early impressionist sketches from *The Left Bank*, especially in such pieces as "Mannequin," the central idea of Rhys's later fiction is virtually complete. Society gives a woman only a limited number of roles to play. She is paid or rewarded only when she plays these roles to perfection. Each of the twelve mannequins in the Parisian dress shop knows her type and keeps to it, "Babbette, the gamine, the traditional blonde enfant: Mona, tall and darkly beautiful, the femme fatale, the wearer of sumptuous evening gowns. Georgette was the garconne . . . " (reprinted in *Tigers Are Better Looking*, 176). At the conclusion to the story there is a surrealistic tinge to the evening as all the mannequins come out of their shops and make the pavement gay as beds of flowers until the girls are swallowed up in the night of Paris.

If a story like "Mannequin" looks ahead to the theme of the later fiction of Rhys, it also looks back to the great dramatic poems of the Victorian period like those in Robert Browning's *Men and Women*. The formula Browning exploits in his dramatic monologues is to create a tension between the reader's sympathy for and judgment of a character. Typically, Browning takes a strongly stereotyped character and gives the reader a view of the inner feelings and motives which contradict the public role the character must play. For this reason, Browning is particularly fond of depicting churchmen who have natural impulses at odds with their public roles, like the Bishop at St. Praxed's, Fra Lippo Lippi, or Bishop Blougram.

Browning's Bishop Blougram explains Browning's strategy of characterization when he asserts that he will always be interesting because he is an enigma, a man who knows about skepticism, yet believes with the faith of a true bishop. How can he reconcile his private cynicism with the public role he plays? Bishop Blougram says that characters like himself will always hold our interest:

The honest thief, the tender murderer,
The superstitious atheist, demirep
That loves and saves her soul in New French books—
We watch while these in equilibrium keep
The giddy line midway: one step aside,
They're classed and done with. I, then, keep the line
Before your sages,—just the men to shrink
From gross weights, coarse scales and labels broad
You offer their refinement. Fool or knave,
Why needs a bishop be a fool or knave
When there's a thousand diamond weights between?

Rhys makes a strong female stereotype the central figure in all her fiction, a mannequin of one kind or another cast in some role thrust on the woman by society. Following the pattern of Robert Browning's dramatic monologues, Rhys lets us into the interior of the character, showing how difficult it is to maintain the stereotype in the light of its painfully contradictory, crossed purposes. For example, Rhys's short story "Illusion" depicts Miss Bruce, tall, thin, a shining example of what "British character and training" can do for a woman. In Paris, surrounded by the cult of beauty and love, she is always severe, sensibly dressed in "neat tweed costume in winter, brown shoes with low heels and cotton stockings" (reprinted in *Tigers Are Better Looking*, 164). Miss Bruce suddenly falls ill, and the narrator of her tale enters her flat to get some necessities for her in hospital. When she opens Miss Bruce's wardrobe, she finds a "glow of colour, a riot of soft silks . . . everything that one did not expect" (reprinted in *Tigers Are Better Looking*, 166). Evidently the clothes are never worn, but indicate that the sensible Miss Bruce is afflicted with "the perpetual hunger to be beautiful and that thirst to be loved which is the real curse of Eve." Miss Bruce is acutely embarrassed to discover that her friend has found her collection of clothes, and she asserts at the conclusion of the story that she never would make such a fool of herself as actually to wear them.

The reader finds Miss Bruce fascinating for exactly the same reasons as Robert Browning's churchmen. How can the Bishop at St. Praxed's, with all his love of luxury and of the pleasures of the senses, play the role of ascetic? How can Miss Bruce, with her streak of feminine longing for soft, bright fabrics, play the role of sensible and severe British woman? The core of such characters is repression. At what cost must Miss Bruce's love for beautiful clothes be repressed? At what cost does Bishop Blougram repress his skepticism or St. Praxed's Bishop his sensuality?

Conrad's Lord Jim, too, is just such a dual character, struggling to repress his fears and anxieties so as to play the role of hero as prescribed by boys' light fiction. The repressive tension produces a split character, a *Doppelgaenger*. As in a morality play, the good or socially approved type struggles against the bad or disapproved tendency. One pole of the character is the repressive type, the other pole is the freedom of personal inclination. Failure to repress the personality results in social ostracism, loss of affection, incarceration, pain, and madness. All of Rhys's heroines are trying to be "good girls," but find it impossible to fit into the stereotype. They are forced to misbehave socially and sexually, to get drunk, to commit all sorts of "excesses" until they are disgraced. If the character opts for personal inclination and disregards the dictates of society's prescribed role for a good girl, she follows the path of Emma Bovary. If she buys the role and represses her deviant tendencies, she follows the model of Jane Eyre. Jane Eyre and the madwoman Antoinette are twins, prim repression versus destructive passion. What can make Rochester turn a blind eye toward the dark side of his woman?

Many readers see Jane Eyre as struggling between rebellion and obedience. As Charlotte Brontë's novel closes, Jane emerges as the heroine of repression, control, and decency. Her dark twin lurking in Rochester's attic is the mad, unrepressed, violent, drunken, licentious West Indian—Jane's black alter ego. Only when the dark woman is burned away, can Jane unite respectably with Rochester. Jane effects her purgation through intense suffering and British schooling, both of which Rhys shows insupportable to Antoinette. Rather than killing the dark, sensual, loose shadow in order to become a prim governess and wife, Antoinette overpowers the white sister's stereotype and rages destructively against the restraints of British customs. No doubt Antoinette, like Emma Bovary, fails to live up to expectations. Nevertheless, she evokes sympathy in the reader of Rhys's text because she questions the cultural assumptions on which the stereotypes of British female decency are built. In the light of Rhys's fiction, the madwoman is the true heroine, like the jazz singer in the punishment cells at Holloway Prison, not the submissive Jane Eyre.

Rhys often writes stories which display deviations from normal perceptions, such as hallucinations induced by extreme pain or suffering, drunkenness, drugs, or madness. In this way she raises questions about what is normal, or what is normative, in the fiction. On what basis does the reader form a judgment about normality versus deviation? For instance, in *Voyage in the Dark*, the heroine is a young West Indian who hates England and is forced to tour the British provinces as a chorus girl to earn a pittance. An older, wealthy Englishman, Walter, keeps her as his mistress. A climax of the novel occurs when the heroine and Walter spend a weekend in the country with his sneering young friend, Vincent, and Vincent's girlfriend, Germaine. They reveal that Walter is about to leave for America for several months. They then ask how old the heroine is and where Walter met her. She replies that she was in a show in Southsea. Vincent jokingly asks Walter what he was doing on a pier in Southsea, and the three English people begin to laugh. The heroine does not understand what they are laughing at. The others ignore her when she asks them to explain the joke. Suddenly, she grinds her lighted cigarette into the back of Walter's hand. The act is as mad and destructive as Antoinette's blinding Rochester by fire. It is also as self-destructive as Antoinette's suicidal arson. From that moment forward, Walter is set on deserting her.

The act of burning Walter's hand, however, seems crazy, socially deviant, savage, only if we do not question the assumptions of the dominant society, only if we assume that the laughter of Walter, Vincent, and Germaine is acceptable aggression; whereas, burning Walter's hand is beyond the limits of reasonable action. The thrust of the story, however, is exactly to question that normative framework. It is not so crazy to burn Walter's hand, it is not really incomprehensible that Antoinette burns Rochester's house, provided we are willing to see things from the alien woman's side.

Literature provides a way to explore the human values embodied in social behavior. When the traditional roles and patterns of behavior available to individuals in a society seem unacceptable, fiction allows us harmlessly to search for new ways to fit our desires to traditional expectations. Many fictions present a character with a possible choice, such as marriage. The character can consider three aspects of the prospective behavior: Is it approved by society? Is it profitable? Is it desired by the character making the choice? If the answer to all three of these questions is, "Yes," there is no need to write a novel. On the other hand, if the answer to one of these questions is, "No," we have the formula generating literally thousands of fictional works which explore how to reconcile approved and profitable behavior with what is desired. Both Charlotte Brontë and Rhys personally lived through this kind of acute conflict between the limited social roles available to them and their contrary desires.

*Wide Sargasso Sea* is not merely a sequel to *Jane Eyre*. Both novels can stand independently as separate works; but, when the two works are taken together in juxtaposition, their meaning is enormously incremented, because both explore the limitations of available social roles, especially for young women, in western culture. As the second term in the juxtaposition of texts, *Wide Sargasso Sea* opens the fiction and forces the reader into a constructive activity, judging and evaluating Jane Eyre's behavior afresh. The reader must engage in the debate and actively decide what set of values to join. So Rhys sets up the impressionist Galvanic current to defamiliarize and to revitalize the text of *Jane Eyre*. The juxtaposition of Charlotte Brontë's Jane Eyre with Rhys's Antoinette increments the meaning of the two characters in the same way as the double exposure in the visual collage of the Viet Nam era photo of a burning Asian baby superimposed on a picture of a Western industrial assembly line, discussed above.

Juxtaposition operates to increment meaning on the small scale, on the level of individual words, as well as on the larger scale of comparing characters and situations in a novel. When sets of identical words recur in a text, sometimes they take on an unexpected vitality, like the incremental repetition found in traditional ballads where each time a refrain recurs it is freighted with new and unexpected meaning. Consider the case of "shoes" in "Heart of Darkness." On the deck of the Nellie in the fictive present time level, Marlow speaks figuratively of stepping "into the shoes" of his dead predecessor, Fresleven the Dane (54). In the events in the Congo, the figurative shoes become concrete and ghastly as the helmsman of Marlow's boat is fatally speared and his blood fills Marlow's shoes. Marlow is "morbidly anxious to change . . . shoes and socks" (113) and flings his shoes overboard. Even though the real reader is perhaps not conscious of the echo or resonant repetition of the word "shoes," the initial bland figurative statement becomes concrete and unbearable as the tale develops. The story unfolds so as to make the reader feel the horror of stepping into the shoes of European imperialists.

The affective tone of "shoes" darkens as the reader proceeds through the text. There is a turbulence created in the reader's mind when the expectation for the word, "shoes," begins as a neutral or benign concept, but the word recurs in more and more sinister contexts. The European reader of English begins to feel that shod versus barefoot, like black versus white, creates opposed communities of value. The text entangles the readers' feet, cased in shoes, displaying the evidence of their community. First "step into the shoes" with Marlow, then "jump into the same boat" with Lord Jim and, like the characters held in contempt by Browning's Bishop Blougram, the readers are "classed and done with."

Consider the sequential string of occurrences of the word "fire" in "Heart of Darkness." "Fire" first occurs in the fictive present on the deck of the Nellie, figuratively. The denominated concept is extremely eulogistic in the utterance of the outer narrator, who praises the impact of English adventurers, "bearing the sword, and often the torch, messengers of the might within the land, bearers of a spark from the sacred fire" (47). Such figurative, eulogistic fire on the fictive present time level becomes dyslogistic as it recurs in the text. The next time the reader encounters the word, it is concrete in the fictive past time level in the Congo; "One evening a grass shed full of calico, cotton prints, beads, and I don't know what else, burst into a blaze so suddenly that you would have thought the earth had opened to let an avenging fire consume all that trash" (76). The avenging, destructive fire in the warehouse, flickers in the eyes of Kurtz (134) and the "savage who was fireman" (97). Like "shoes," the civilized figurative "fire" becomes more threatening and solid as the reader travels through the text.

Attitudes attached to words often modulate with little or no conscious awareness on the part of the reader as he or she proceeds through the text. When Ford discusses his search with Conrad for *le mot juste*, he probably wants to select lexical items so as to create exactly such experience of shifting connotation. Ford's *le mot juste* generates a sense of authentic turbulence in the reader's lexicon. Setting the same word in a string of contexts compels the reader to adjust and modify the concept signified each time the signifier recurs.

Such a series of recurring words triggers a modulation, a shifting, a feeling of instability about the preconceptions which the reader brings initially to the vocabulary used in the text.

Affective modulation or turbulence appears to be an important part of the reading process, linking past to present time levels, linking outer to inner story tellers in twice-told tales, linking frame to core situations in a single text. Similar lexical turbulence can also exist between separate texts. Rhys's *Wide Sargasso Sea*, like Charlotte Brontë's *Jane Eyre*, is a female *bildungsroman* or novel depicting the development, the metamorphosis, or the modulation of character from childhood toward some decisive, adult act. Rhys in *Wide Sargasso Sea* mirrors the pattern of events in *Jane Eyre*, depicting her heroine first in her childhood home, then in her school years, then in her sexual awakening to the allure of Rochester. In addition to the generally parallel movement of the plot in the sequence of events shaping the development of Jane Eyre and that of Antoinette Cosway, there is a similar modulation in recurring denominated concepts in the two texts.

In *Jane Eyre* the word "fire" is often eulogistic, associated with warmth, comfort, and security opposed to ice and coldness. For example, as a child, she faints in fear, but awakes in a terrible red glare, only to realize that it is the light of the warm nursery fire and that she is being cared for by Mr. Loyd and Bessie (see beginning of Chapter 3, concordance 26.19). "Fire" is associated with feeling, passion, and emotion, which can be dangerous as well as beneficial. At the dyslogistic extreme, Mr. Brocklehurst quizzes Jane, "And what is Hell? Can you tell me that?" Jane replies, "A pit full of fire" (54.10). The text of the novel leads the reader through a series of affective modulations associated with the word "fire."

*Jane Eyre* opposes fire and ice, blaze and darkness, passion and restraint, imagination and drab reality. At Thornfield Hall Jane tells us her imagination narrated to her a tale "quickened with all of incident, life, *fire*, feeling, that I desired and had not in my actual existence" (216.01-05, emphasis added). "Bright visions" in her imagination "glow" and make her "heart heave." These imaginative fluctuations are replicated in the flickering flames of the repeated references to "fire" in the text.

The fearful red room at Gateshead where Mr. Reed had died is marked by its chill and the absence of any fire (16.13). But a warm fire is often a source of light, consolation, and comfort for Jane (26.19, 46.14, 71.13, 73.03, 76.06, 113.17, 175.20, 181.14, 185.27, 186.07, 186.24, 187.11, 457.08, 461.28, 562.03, 562.06). At Jane's Lowood school, Miss Miller and, especially, Miss Temple glow in firelight (85.10, 134.06, 137.13, 138.24, 139.09). When Helen Burns is punished by wearing a sign declaring that she is a "slattern," Jane throws the sign into a fire (141.20). When the fire and candle burn out, Jane is filled with dread (29.08). Bessie asks Jane not to cry, but she might as well have commanded fire not to burn (33.25). Brocklehurst and others tell Jane to fear Hell's fire (54.10, 57.23). Mr. Rochester's ancestral home, Thornfield Hall, is described in its glasswork and mirrors as a magical "blending of snow and fire" (204.19).

When Jane first meets Rochester, he falls from his horse so that he apparently needs her help. She speculates that, if Rochester had been a handsome youth, she would have shunned him "as one would fire, lightning, or anything else that is bright but antipathetic" (225.03). On the other hand, Rochester's home has a "genial fire in the grate" (231.10) and Rochester basks in a luxurious, "superb fire" (236.27, 237.03, 258.14, 259.04, 259.11, 276.07). The master summons Jane to "come to the fire" and join him (240.22). He wants to add her companionship to the warmth of his fire (263.12, 567.09). As Jane warms to Rochester, his face becomes for her "more cheering than the brightest fire" (292.13). Rochester's brain is inflamed by Jane (586.01).

Is Jane playing with fire? Jane discovers the curtains of Rochester's bed mysteriously ablaze. She rescues him from the fire (296.10, 297.09, 298.07, 307.21). Now there is a strange fire in Rochester's look, after his escape from the burning bed (302.04).

When neighboring gentry visit Thornfield, the general disarray in the household is expressed by the panic in the kitchen by the cooking fire (334.18. 334.24). For the guests the house is made warm and bright (341.02, 342.28, 384.06). Mr. Mason, recently arrived in England from the West Indies, is constantly cold and demands more coals be poured on the fire (385.02, 411.06). When Rochester plays the gypsy fortune teller and cruelly teases Jane, he is next to the fire (398.08). As he, in the guise of the gypsy woman, advises Jane to grasp her fortune, she begs to be let go for "the fire scorches me" (404.03), even as Rochester sees it flame in her eyes. Jane asserts that despite strong wind, earthquake, and fire, she will be guided only by her conscience (405.20). When Jane stirs the fire, it illuminates the gypsy woman's hand (406.22). When Antoinette wounds Mr. Mason, in the general alarm Jane asks if there is a fire (416.04). So the mystery in the house seems to Jane to be expressed in fire and blood (424.16). Rochester tells Jane that he stands over a crater which might spew fire at any moment (436.14).

Rochester tells Jane that he can never love an insipid, merely pretty woman, but that a "soul made of fire" inspires him (528.07). His weird courtship promises to light Jane's fire (540.24, 540.25). When Jane's wedding with Rochester is interrupted by the revelation that Rochester already has a mad wife confined in the attic of Thornfield Hall, Jane's blood turns to fire and ice (592.08). Rochester feels the pain of "quenchless fire," at the inhibition of his bigamous plan to marry Jane (596.17). When Jane rejects the idea of becoming Rochester's mistress, she fixes her eyes on the fire and her veins run with fire (619.02, 648.16). When she finally rejects Rochester's illicit proposal, his eyes flash fire (651.15).

After the humiliation of her interrupted marriage, Jane flees from Rochester and takes refuge with the Rivers family. There she hears Mary and Diana read powerful, emotional lines in German, while gazing deep into the fire (678.15). As they take pity on Jane and give her food and comfort, Diana's long curls come between Jane and the fire (685.28). The warmth of their home is displayed by its genial fire (688.06, 693.05), but Jane must be careful not to become overheated (700.15). When St. John Rivers displays emotion, Jane sees "his solemn eye melt with sudden fire" (740.27). Rosamond Oliver is attracted to St. John Rivers and imagines her heart sacrificed in the fire of a holy altar (747.12). On the other hand, Jane dreams "with force and fire" of being united with Rochester (745.23). When St. John Rivers is absent, a snowstorm reduces Jane's fire (765.08), but when he enters her home he approaches the fire and stands in fire-light (766.17, 767.10) He asks Jane to come nearer to the fire (769.26). "I am hot and fire dissolves ice," Jane says as St. John reveals to her that they are cousins and that she is an heiress (778.25). St. John Rivers proposes that Jane become his wife and share in his missionary work. She imagines her life as his wife, "Always restrained, and always checked—-forced to keep the fire of my nature continually low, to compel it to burn inwardly and never utter a cry, though the imprisoned flame consumed vital after vital—-this would be unendurable" (826.01). Jane feels the torturing fire of indignation (832.19). St. John Rivers makes a sermon for Jane, reminiscent of Mr. Brocklehurst's earlier threats, fearing that she will fall "in the lake which burneth with fire and brimstone" (844.21).

Jane hears a supernatural cry summoning her to return to Rochester and, leaving the Rivers family, she finds that Rochester's Thornfield Hall has been destroyed by fire (861.22). As the garrulous inn keeper tells Jane about the fire, he digresses to repeat the story of how deeply Rochester was in love with the young governess formerly at Thornfield. Jane tries to direct his tale to the arson, saying, "But the fire" (862.25). The fire of Rochester's passion and the destructive fire at Thornfield intertwine as he tells the tale. The madwoman in the attic, the West Indian wife of Rochester, set the fire (863.14, 864.05). Rochester lost his sight and his hand in the fire (865.13). When Jane meets Rochester again, he is sitting by a neglected fire (874.24). He bears the scar of fire (881.16). Jane makes a comforting fire for him and, although blind, he says he can dimly see its glow in one eye (881.25, 881.26). Rochester tells Jane how dreary his life has been without her, so that he let the fire go out (883.23). When Rochester and Jane are finally married, the announcement is made in the kitchen as a pair of chickens are roasting on a cheerful, domestic fire (905.18).

Francis Hueffer, the father of Ford Madox (Hueffer) Ford, was an early champion of Richard Wagner (1813-1883) and his music. Patterns of recurrent imagery, designated by repeated vocabulary, where each recurrence of the keyword requires some adjustment of the readers' affective response, resembles Wagner's use of *leitmotif*. The experience of reading a novel, like the experience of hearing a Wagnerian opera performed, includes more than merely following the characterization and plot. A rich texture of recurring themes, often operating below the level of conscious awareness, bundle together affective responses, like the example of fire and ice in *Jane Eyre*. The enhanced reading environment provided by computer-generated concordances and word lists makes it possible to highlight these sensitive sets of denominated concepts and bring into the readers' consciousness the fluctuation of feeling generated by recurrent words.

Light versus dark, heat versus cold, items of clothing, animals, enclosures and thresholds, body parts like "hand" or "foot," repeated gestures, sets of colors, and similar groups of words blend together in the text over and above the more obvious elements of the story, such as definition of the characters and the sequence of their actions forming the plot. Sometimes the tonal texture contradicts the plot, sometimes it reinforces it. Consider the example of "lightning" in *Jane Eyre*: When Rochester first kisses Jane, the storm of their emotions is expressed by a storm in nature as lightning crashes and thunder echoes (520.05). In the reflection of cold dawn, however, Jane learns that the lightning has destroyed a great tree in the orchard (520.15), coloring the joy of her passion with a threatening overtone.

The leitmotif engages the reader in an authentic activity. The reader's self (autos) must dwell in the text, for the text is made up of bundles of responses to repeatedly denominated concepts. The reader is required to respond personally to recurrent words, "Is this a genial fire or a dangerous fire? Is lightning a joyous expression of sexual union or is it a fearful, destructive force of nature?" The response is the impression of each reader. The affective tone of a fictional episode, the emotional blending or coloring of each scene, depends on the way the attitude of the reader modulates or shifts with each recurrence of the signifier.

When Rhys created *Wide Sargasso Sea*, she expanded the characters in Charlotte Brontë's *Jane Eyre*, filling in the almost blank identity of Antoinette Cosway, the madwoman in the attic, and making Rochester much more rounded and complex. Rhys also imitated the sequence of events initially developed by Charlotte Brontë so as to create a parallel *bildungsroman*. *Jane Eyre* depicts the harsh girlhood of Jane with the Reed family at Gateshead, her repressive and harsh schooling at Lowood, followed by her sexual encounter with Rochester at Thornfield Hall. *Wide Sargasso Sea* repeats that sequence of events in the life of Antoinette: her frightened childhood at Coulibri, her convent schooling, and her disastrous sexual involvement with Rochester. But over and above the parallel in character and plot between *Jane Eyre* and *Wide Sargasso Sea*, Rhys adopts in her text the bundle of repeated imagery, the network of leitmotifs from Charlotte Brontë's work.

Consider, for example, the tonal modulation of fire and ice in *Wide Sargasso Sea*. Antoinette's home Coulibri is burned by rebellious blacks (39). They burn the crib of her mentally defective brother, Pierre, who dies as a result of the attack. Her pet parrot Coco dies with its feathers aflame (43) in the attack on Coulibri. One of the former slaves says, "Black and white, they burn the same" (44). In *Jane Eyre* the nasty cousin, John Reed, wounds Jane by hurling a book at her head. In *Wide Sargasso Sea* Antoinette's cruel black playmate, Tia, injures Antoinette's head by hurling a rock at her (45). Jane attends Lowood school; Antoinette the convent school where she cross stitches her name "in fire red, Antoinette Mason, née Cosway, Mount Calvary Convent, Spanish Town, Jamaica, 1839" (53). The convent is her "refuge, a place of sunshine, and of death" (56).

Rochester arrives in Jamaica and soon burns with a fever (67). On his honeymoon at Coulibri, a large moth flies into the candle on the dinner table and is burned (81). Later, as the accusations against Antoinette grow in Rochester's mind, "the procession of small moths and beetles fly into the candle flames" (126). And, of course, the conclusion of both *Jane Eyre* and *Wide Sargasso Sea* (188) is a pyrotechnical extravaganza as the madwoman in the attic burns the house down around herself and Rochester.

Rhys elaborates the patterns of imagery found in Charlotte Brontë's work, as well as the characterization and the plot of *Jane Eyre*. Rhys succeeds in condensing the image of fire into a few concentrated instances: the great houses at Coulibri and Thornfield consumed in flames; the parrot Coco falling with blazing feathers, the moths and insects drawn to the candle; the fire of passion and imagination; and the incandescent death of the madwoman who tries to escape from her confinement.

Both Charlotte Brontë and Rhys create cognitive dissonance by setting up competing frames for repeated motifs. The well-known picture of "Rabbit or Duck," shown in the illustration below, can be read as one animal or the other, but not both rabbit and duck at the same time.

The design of "Rabbit or Duck" facetiously illustrates the tension which can be created when two competing frames struggle for control of a single signifier. A more serious example of such tension appears in Henri Matisse's painting "Harmony in Red/La Desserte" dated 1908 and currently in The Hermitage Museum, St. Petersburg. *La Desserte* normally would mean the small table in a dining room to hold the dessert course. This canvas is mainly a flat dark red surface decorated with a large scale, deep blue floral design. There is a predominantly green square in the upper left corner of the picture. The first impression of the canvas is probably, as its title indicates, that it is an abstract exercise or a "Harmony in Red." Closer examination quickly shows, however, that the green square in the upper left corner is perhaps a window looking out to a distant blooming orchard with three white blossomed trees, that there is a cane bottomed chair positioned in front of the window partially off the canvas at the left edge. The center of the picture, upon closer inspection, is not a flat plane, but displays a table projecting at right angles to the wall, although the table cloth on the table picks up the colors and the floral design on the wall so smoothly that it is difficult to define exactly where the edge of the table lies. If we accept a three dimensional frame for reading the picture, we can see that there may be two decanters, two fruit dishes, and some stray pieces of fruit on the table. Finally, on the right edge of the canvas, there is the figure of a woman in a white apron arranging fruit on one of the dishes, perhaps making the dessert, as suggested in the second half of the title of the painting. The artistic energy of this picture comes from the tension the viewer feels between reading the canvas as a flat plane and the demand that the table must thrust out at right angles to the wall so as to create a plausible space in which the figure of the woman can exist. The green square in the upper left might be a window opening deep into space beyond the wall. On the other hand, it might be a flat picture hanging on the wall. The viewer is caught in a contradictory ambiguity when reading this canvas similar to that of the "Rabbit or Duck" design.

Rhys in *Wide Sargasso Sea* creates a similar, systematic ambiguity in her repetition of "fire." When we encounter a fire, is it warm, genial, imaginative, and passionate in a life-affirming way, or is it destructive, painful, punitive, frightening, and death dealing? Caught in the tension between ambiguous responses, the reader must actively decide which set of values dominates. The selfhood of the reader enters into the creation of the text. Such participation of the audience in the construction of the experience of art differentiates "authentic" art from "inauthentic." The inauthentic experience of art is passive. The inauthentic audience is not engaged in the production of the experience. The meaning of the inauthentic artifact is predetermined and closed. In an authentic experience of art, the audience participates actively in the creation. Each viewer constructs a unique experience. The values brought by each "self" in the audience shape how the artifact is read. No two readings are the same. The perceptive eye creates the authentic experience.

Yet, Rochester must be blinded by the fire. Why? Is Rochester paying for his hubris, like King Oedipus, who blinds himself when he finally sees what the sun god Apollo reveals to him? Is Christophine a voodoo Tiresias accurately prophesying that Rochester will lose his eyesight when he sees the truth? In *Joseph Conrad: A Personal Remembrance*, Ford entitles Part III of the four parts of his text, "It is before all things to make you *see*," quoting one of Conrad's key statements about fiction. Conrad and Ford were keen on showing, rather than telling. Instead of making a moral pronouncement about a fictional scene, the impressionist simply shows the scene and forces the reader to draw his or her own conclusions. As Ford says, "Seeing is believing for all the doubters of this planet, from Thomas to the end: if you can make humanity see the few very simple things upon which this temporal world rests you will make mankind believe such eternal truths as are universal" (JC 168). Fiction like sight should be immediate, vivid, and should avoid imposing the author's judgments on the gentle reader, according to Ford.

Yet the trope of *sight*, like that of *fire*, is ambiguous. On many levels, Conrad's privileging of sight is characteristic of the impressionist position. What is presented to the eyes appears to be immediate and certain experience, while the interpretation or evaluation of that experience is produced by subsequent ratiocination, which is subject to error. Marlow in the attack on his riverboat sees immediately little sticks flying thickly through the air, only later he concludes that they are "Arrows, by Jove." The belief that reading a text should resemble seeing an object creates an extremely powerful, but questionable, metaphor at the center of the modernist movement in literature.

What if we were to reverse the sequence of events in *Jane Eyre* and in *Wide Sargasso Sea* so that a blind Rochester is restored to sight. What if Jane first meets Rochester blinded and then she has to adjust to his miraculous restoration of sight in a blaze at the center of which the dark Antoinette works her witchcraft? In that case, Jane would be confronted with the *Molyneux Question* as outlined in John Locke's (1632-1704) *An Essay Concerning Human Understanding* (1694). Molyneux asks what would actually happen in the case of restored sight. What might we suppose would occur when the heroic prisoner in Plato's allegory of the cave first emerges into the full light of the sun. Specifically, Locke proposes that a man born blind learns to distinguish by touch between a sphere and a cube. If his sight is restored and he looks for the first time at a sphere and a cube, could he tell which was which by sight alone. Molyneux and Locke say "no," for there must be some prior linking of the tactile experience to the visual experience. There must be some constructive judgment made in the mind before we are able to register visual impressions.

Ford and Conrad were not technically well-trained philosophers. Their engagement with the problem of how impressions impinge on the mind is intuitive and practical in nature, arising from the actual practice of writing books. In Conrad's "Arrows, by Jove!" scene it seems that Conrad begins with Marlow's idea of "arrows" and then tries to trace that conception back to its initial roots in particular sensory experience. Yet, in the characteristics of impressionist narrative such as limited, unreliable narration; fragmentation, defamiliarization, and incremental juxtaposition in collage; turbulence and cognitive dissonance created through repeated leitmotif; Conrad and Ford pull away from the idea that language is a transparent statement *about* experience. The main contribution of Rhys to the development of the impressionist line of thought is enormously to heighten the notion that language triggers a constructive activity. Each interpretive act is unique, contingent, and temporary. Authentic aesthetic experience is the ongoing, shimmering, constructive process of reading.

Unnamed "Privileged Person"

Marlow's Story

Jim

French Lieutenant

German Stein

Brierly's Officer Jones

Et Al.

Epistle

# CHAPTER V
## COMMUNITY OF VALUE: HERO AND CLOWN

*Formation of communities of value. Pseudo-speciation. Impressionist internalization of the Romance Quest: Hemingway, Conrad, and Ford on heroism. Social integration and alienation. The comic sense of Conrad, Ford, and Rhys. Corrective versus subversive laughter. Henry Fielding's theory of the ridiculous. The fragile mask. Incongruous juxtapositions and laughable loves. Henri Bergson on laughter: mechanical incrustation on the vital elan.*

Conrad's "Heart of Darkness" or *Lord Jim*, Ford's *The Good Soldier* or parts of his Tietjens Tetralogy, and Rhys's *Wide Sargasso Sea* all display limited or "unreliable" narration. In each text, the story is told through the limitations of one or more characters so that what the story teller asserts does not always agree with the readers' understanding of the tale. For example, we might imagine a story set up so that a thief tells of his crime and asserts that he is a terribly clever fellow. At the end of the work, however, he is arrested and punished. Such a tale sets up a contrast between showing and telling. The limited intelligence of the speaker *tells* us that he is clever, but the work as a whole *shows* us that he is not. Because the speaker in such a case is limited, obtuse, or "unreliable," we say that he is not so privileged as the author's own voice might be. Literary critics speak of the degree of privilege a speaker has in fictional narrative, meaning the degree of divergence the reader perceives between the ideas and attitudes expressed by the speaker and the "authorial intention" or normative judgment implied by the author in the total work.

Conrad's *Lord Jim* is a particularly interesting example of varying degrees of privilege in limited narration. The central affair, the disgraceful abandonment of the pilgrim ship Patna by the young officer, Jim, is the subject of a hearing by a court of inquiry. Conrad's limited narrator, Marlow, witnesses the proceedings and organizes what he thinks he knows about Jim into a story. The text therefore is a twice-told tale. Various witnesses tell Marlow; Marlow tells the story as he sees it to a group of listeners on a veranda on a certain evening; one member of that audience presumably tells us the words which make up the total text of the novel, augmented particularly by a packet of documents addressed to the "privileged" story teller (so designated in the text at 434.27 and 416.17). The narrative is a series of nested "unreliable" statements. Can the reader trust the individual witnesses? Can we trust Marlow? Can we trust the "outer" narrator who reports Marlow's speech to us? At what level in this scheme does truth reside?

*Lord Jim* is written as an impressionist affair. The core of the story is a scandalous event which has already taken place when the narrative opens: Jim, the British officer, apparently fear-stricken for his own safety, abandoned his ship and passengers following an accident at sea. In the lifeboat, the other craven officers plan to tell the authorities that their ship has sunk without trace and that they are its sole survivors. A French ship, however, comes upon the floating derelict, places a French Lieutenant on board, and tows the wreck and its passengers safely to port. The narrative proceeds in ever-growing circles of complexity as the reader tries to understand Jim's character. The reader's initial guess that he is a simple coward, or simply irresponsible, is not nearly adequate to explain the whole affair.

The dramatic tension of the story lies not in the events, but in the contrast between the various observers' impressions of those events: the French lieutenant's mind contrasted to Jim's; Marlow the story teller's impression played against that of the privileged person in his audience who relays the story to us.

We might visualize the simplified scheme of "nested unreliable" or twice-told narration in *Lord Jim* in the following illustration:

Marlow, the story teller, collects documentation from informants and his own eyewitness, quotes these sources, and shapes a story which he tells to an audience on a certain evening. A member of that audience, the unnamed "privileged person" or outer narrator, reports what Marlow says and adds information to which he alone is privy from a letter and a few other sources, thus creating the total text of the fiction as we have it.

Since English was not Conrad's mother tongue and he wrote English laboriously, we might expect to find a high proportion of foreign words in his novels. In fact, Conrad seems very careful to keep non-English words segregated for special uses in his text. *Table I* and *Table II*, below, give a summary of the French and German vocabulary employed in Conrad's *Lord Jim*.

## Table I
### French Vocabulary in Conrad's *Lord Jim*

| | | | |
|---|---|---|---|
| allez | 178.17 | lachez | 178.26 |
| au | 176.04 | la | 178.20 |
| autour | 169.14 | les | 169.28, 177.16 |
| autres | 177.16 | marins | 173.10 |
| bien | 170.29, 171.20, 178.21, | ménagements | 169.29 |
| | 178.22, 174.12 | merci | 168.23, 170.27, 171.21 |
| bosse | 178.14 | métier | 178.20 |
| c'est | 171.20 | mon | 174.07 |
| ca | 171.20, 178.20, 181.02 | monde | 173.08 |
| cadavre | 167.12, 173.11 | monsieur | 180.27, 181.03, 181.15, 181.24 |
| cassis | 169.04 | ne | 179.24, 180.24 |
| ce | 167.21, 169.14, 171.04, 173.08 | notez | 170.29 |
| cet | 173.11, 173.21 | ouvrir | 171.28 |
| comprendre | 169.06 | parbleu | 169.17, 179.08, 179.25 |
| concevez | 169.06 | pas | 180.24 |
| coquet | 175.12 | peut | 171.05 |
| d'hôte | 243.02 | qu'on | 171.04 |
| dans | 173.21 | qualité | 170.16 |
| de | 169.06, 169.14, 170.16, | que | 173.20, 179.03 |
| | 172.20, 173.10, 173.20 | s'en | 171.20 |
| diable | 179.03 | s'est | 177.16 |
| dieu | 170.27, 174.0 | sans | 170.15 |
| doute | 170.15 | serviteur | 181.23 |
| enfin | 172.03 | seul | 180.24 |
| enfue | 177.16 | sorte | 173.20 |
| entendue | 178.23 | tout | 173.08, 178.26, 180.24 |
| épouvantable | 178.29 | toute | 169.22 |
| est | 179.24 | trés | 175.22 |
| état | 173.10 | triste | 175.24 |
| exigeait | 169.28 | va | 171.20 |
| fait | 171.04 | veux | 178.20 |
| finis | 215.03, 215.11 | vie | 173.22 |
| juste | 176.04 | vient | 180.24 |
| l' | 173.10 | ville | 175.24 |
| l'eau | 169.04 | voilà | 179.27 |
| l'homme | 179.24 | vôtre | 170.16 |
| l'oeil | 171.28 | vous | 169.06, 178.25 |

## Table II
### German Vocabulary in Conrad's *Lord Jim*

| | | | |
|---|---|---|---|
| Ach | 241.17, 258.09, | ich's | 257.03 |
| | 259.17, 428.19, | ist | 241.21, 241.22 |
| | 433.21 | Ja | 259.14, 260.19 |
| Bleibt | 256.04 | mein | 125.01, 133.29, |
| denn | 257.03 | | 257.04 |
| ein | 241.21, 241.22 | meinen | 257.03 |
| endlich | 257.03 | nenn' | 257.04 |
| ewig | 261.29 | nicht | 260.29 |
| ewigheit | 55.25 | residenz' | 254.04 |
| ganz | 256.04 | ruhig | 256.05 |
| gelungen | 255.17 | schon | 268.02 |
| gewiss | 263.21 | schrecklich | 432.30 |
| gewissen | 257.04 | schwein | 27.04 |
| gott, *etc.* | 122.15, 125.01, | sehen | 429.02 |
| | 133.30, 260.21 | sie | 429.02 |
| halt' | 257.03 | sinne | 257.04 |
| himmel | 260.21 | und | 257.04 |
| idee | 241.21, 241.22 | verfluchte | 49.13 |

While the concordance to *Lord Jim* shows a fairly extensive vocabulary in French and German (see *Table I* and *Table II* above), except for the trivial case of *d'hôte* and *finis*, all the French words fall between pages 168 and 181 of the text, or in 13 out of the 516 total pages in the novel. The German vocabulary similarly clusters almost entirely in three sections: pages 122-33, 241-68, and 428-33.   Readers of *Lord Jim* do not need a concordance to tell them that Conrad uses foreign words to differentiate character, so that the French words are used entirely in connection with the French Lieutenant, the German words in connection with the four German characters in the story: on pages 122-33 in relation to the cowardly captain of the Patna; pages 241-68 with reference to the businessman Siegmund Yucker, the hotel keeper Schomberg, and the butterfly collector Stein who arranges for Jim's final and fatal job as agent in Patusan; and in the final section in pages 428-33, entirely in relation to Stein.

The French Lieutenant differs from Marlow in the way he sees Jim's desertion of the Patna. Jim's betrayal of duty is unimaginable to the French officer,

> Glancing with one eye into the tumbler, [the French lieutenant] shook his head slightly. 'Impossible de comprendre—vous concevez,' he said with a curious mixture of unconcern and thoughtfulness. I could easily conceive how impossible it had been for them to understand. (169.04-169.09)

Throughout this passage, the *I voice* is Marlow, who imagines all too well how Jim was compelled against all his training to jump from the wrecked ship. The French officer's mind is of a completely different quality, lacking imagination and incapable of sharing Marlow's impression of Jim's act. The use of French words differentiates the characters and separates their conflicting views of Jim's conduct.

Likewise, the German words used by the despicable captain of the Patna indicate that he differs completely from Marlow or Jim in his basic values and orientation. For instance, the German captain, unlike the British officer, Jim, has no respect for the seaman's certificate of competency. The Captain and Jim both lose their papers entitling them to serve as ship's officers as a result of their misconduct, which is a terrible disgrace in Marlow's eyes. The German captain says, "'A man like me don't want your *verfluchte* certificate. I shpit on it.' He spat. 'I vill an American citizen begome'" (49.13-49.15). Here, not only the German word *verfluchte*, but also the phonetic representation of dialect, *shpit, vill, Amerikan,* and *begome,* differentiate Conrad's comic stereotype of the German mind from the decent ideas of the British seaman Marlow.

An important convention in Conrad's narrative is that *authority is granted more readily to a speaker who uses standard or formal English than to one who deviates from it.* When linguistic verisimilitude appears in the text, using foreign words and phrases, slang, phonetic spelling, non-standard or informal discourse, the reader conventionally does not take the values so stated with the same authority as when the language follows formal, standard usage.

Dialect (like *cap'n* or *gabasidy*), slang (like *b'gosh* or *crakee*), phonetic representation (like *d—d—die* or *g—g—glad*), ejaculations (like *oh* or *pah*), as well a foreign vocabulary, in the text of *Lord Jim* seem to call into question the authority of the speaker, inviting the reader to judge for himself or herself what appears to be the case and not to take the speaker's word for it.

Often such deviant forms indicate a highly "dramatized" scene, depicted as if unrolling right before ours eyes, rather than at a distance in past time. Likewise, the use of the apostrophe, creating forms such as *hadn't* for *had not* or *haven't* for *have not* cluster in *Lord Jim* in those sections of the text which are most highly dramatized, which imitate speechways directly. The apostrophe disappears almost entirely as the speaker approaches an authorial voice. When apostrophes occur thickly, in general, the reader *judges* the values expressed by the speaker. When language becomes more formal, the reader *accepts* less critically what the speaker asserts.

Conrad uses linguistic verisimilitude and dialect to control the reader's response to his language, the degree to which the reader accepts the ideas and values of the speaker. The shifting degrees of formality in Conrad's language cause the reader to move in and out of sympathy with the speaker. A mediocre joke of the mid-sixties concerned the Lone Ranger and his faithful companion Tonto. Finding themselves surrounded by fierce Apaches in overwhelming numbers, the Lone Ranger said to Tonto, "Well, we are certainly in a tight spot this time." As the arrows whizzed past them, Tonto replied, "What you mean *we*, white man?" The nub of this story lies in the sudden and surprising regrouping of the characters' allegiances, which is indicated by subtle shifts in language. Under what conditions will a character show allegiance to a particular community of interests or, on the other hand, violate its codes?

Conrad said in his prefaces that his novels are all concerned with simple virtues like *fidelity* and *honor*, and so they are. Marlow says that he must explore Jim's conduct because they both belong to "an obscure body of men held together by a community of inglorious toil and by fidelity to a certain standard of conduct" (59.15-17). But Conrad's fiction is not like *Tom Brown's Schooldays*, merely propaganda for the prescribed set of schoolboy values such as "playing the game fairly" and "never tattling or complaining to authorities," the ethical system of the English public schoolboy as described by Christopher Tietjens with "the love of truth . . . and the belief Arnold forced upon Rugby that the vilest of sins—the vilest of all sins—is to peach to the head master" (PE 490). Conrad's texts force the reader to inquire how such a community of values is formed, what is the basis for elementary social groupings: "What you mean *we*, white man?"

Conrad uses the word *we* in *Lord Jim* 189 times. These 189 tokens can be divided into several obviously different groups. Sometimes *we* signifies a group of characters who *act* together. In other cases, the word *we* designates a group who *agree* in ideas, feelings, or shared experiences. For example, the first use of *we* in *Lord Jim* occurs when one of the boys on Jim's training ship tells how they rescued a drowning sailor in an adventure which Jim had failed to join. The lad says, " . . . the other one, the big one with the beard. When *we* pulled him in he groaned" (8.12). Here the speaker uses the word *we* to indicate that he is part of a group which has *acted* together. Jim listens, eaten with envy and remorse, because he is not part of this group. The word *we* excludes him, while forming a group of co-agents.

Contrast the use of *we* by the story teller when Jim is described as replying to the "odious and fleshy figure" of the German skipper, which "fixed itself in his memory forever as the incarnation of everything vile and base that lurks in the world *we* love: in our own hearts *we* trust for our salvation in the men that surround us" (24.23-25). In this passage, the *we* group is formed by a community of feelings, not of action, and the speaker reaches into the story to include Jim and outward from the story to include the implied reader in Jim's community, while excluding the skipper. The use of *we* in such cases draws the reader into the community of values created by the speaker. If the real reader is hesitant about accepting that community, or adopting those feelings as his own, there is a turbulence between the sets of value created in the fiction and those of the reader. The activity of reading *Lord Jim* creates a struggle between the speakers and their audiences to find an acceptable community of shared values.

Similarly, in the opening paragraphs of "Heart of Darkness," the outer narrator, in what most readers find a comic overstatement, fulsomely celebrates the

English virtues of the "great knights-errant of the sea" whose exploits had carried the "dreams of men, the seeds of commonwealths, the germs of empire" outward from the mouth of the Thames, a river which was in 1899 for all to see grossly polluted and poisonous. At this point in the narrative, the sky darkens in the coming night leaving a "lurid glare" in the sky to mark the "monstrous town," London, upriver and Marlow speaks for the first time, "And this also . . . has been one of the dark places of the earth" (HD 48). In this scene, the ignorant imperial optimism of the outer narrator conflicts with the better informed, more pessimistic attitude of Marlow. The reader perhaps agrees initially as the outer narrator begins his praise for exporting English might and glory, but Marlow's story forces the reader to shift allegiance.

*Lord Jim*, also, actively engages the reader in rejecting or joining communities of value. Lord Jim's version of what happened after he abandoned the Patna at the urging of the other, cowardly, officers shows that the novel constitutes elementary social groupings based on shared values. The other officers are afraid that Jim will tell the truth, if they are rescued, and their story about abandoning a sinking ship will be exposed as a lie. They ask one another, "What can he do?" Jim reports that he thought, "What could I do? Weren't *we* all in the same boat?" (LJ 152.16). The central question of the novel is: even though Jim jumped into the same boat with the craven officers, does he share in the community of values of these men.

Whose community claims Jim? When Marlow first sees Jim, he expects that they belong to the same group:

> I liked his appearance; I knew his appearance; he came from the right place; he was one of us. He stood there for all the parentage of his kind, for men or women by no means clever or amusing, but whose very existence is based upon honest faith, and upon the instinct of courage. (50.20-26)

The central issue of the novel is whether or not Jim finally belongs to Marlow's community or to some other.

A main topic in *Lord Jim* is called *pseudo-speciation* by Erik H. Erikson in *Childhood and Society* (1951). Briefly stated, the theory is that a community's values become ritualized in religion, games, and art. Education frequently consists of acquiring familiarity with those rituals and accepting them. Such a process fortifies one's sense of belonging, but it has the sinister effect of excluding from the community that part of mankind which does not know the proper rituals of behavior. In an extreme form, *pseudo-speciation* allows Hollywood cowboys to kill Indians without paining the feelings of children at Saturday cinema matinees and, when those children grow older, it sometimes happens that they "waste gooks" without remorse.

When Jim abandons the Patna with its crowd of Moslem Pilgrims, Conrad explores for us a paradox of *pseudo-speciation*. The more firmly Jim belongs to the community of Marlow's White Men, the more inhuman his pilgrim cargo seems to him; but the key to belonging to Marlow's community is a paternalistic fidelity to protecting the despised dependent group.

A major, although undenominated, concern in the novel *Lord Jim* is the formation of elementary communities of value. The language of the novel reinforces that topic because it engages the reader in the activity of joining or rejecting such groupings. In the dramatic situation, the reader must decide whether to enlist in the community with Marlow, or with the French Lieutenant, or with the German skipper. Repeatedly the storytelling persona reaches out of the story and tries to draw the reader into a set of values:

> We wander in our thousands over the face of the earth, the illustrious and the obscure, earning beyond the seas our fame, our money, or only a crust of bread; but it seems to me that for each of us going home must be like going to render an account. We return to face our superiors, our kindred, our friends—Those whom we obey, and those whom we love. (270.28-271.05)

The reader has to ask the same question that Jim does, "What do you mean *we*, White Man?"

The fiction is so constructed that the reader is forced to enact the same process in reading the text as the character, Jim, enacts in the plot. Jim's search for his true identity, his proper emotional homeland, becomes the quest of the reader. The reader enters the text on a quest very similar to Jim's in the perilous domain of the mysterious East. Jim crosses the threshold into unknown territory so as prove his heroic virtue, to show that he belongs to the noble company of officers and gentlemen, that he can bear the certificate of maritime competence. Like Robert Browning's Childe Roland, Jim seeks the Dark Tower where his heroic virtue will be tested.

One of the major contributions of the impressionist novel is its internalization of the traditional Romance Quest. From *Sir Gawain and the Green Knight* to Hemingway's *A Farewell to Arms*, the quest pattern forms the basic structure of many narratives: The setting of the physical quest juxtaposes in space two domains, one safe and homely, the other perilous and uncanny. A domain (related to Latin "dominare") is a space governed by a single set of rules. The rules change when we cross the threshold from one domain to another. Often the true object of the quest is to find out what are the strange rules governing the perilous domain.

In *Sir Gawain and the Green Knight*, for example, Sir Gawain's home domain of the court of King Arthur and his knights contrasts with the perilous, weird domain of the forest where the Green Giant dwells. Sir Gawain crosses the threshold from his home domain into the fearful domain of the Green Giant, where his heroic virtue is tested. Likewise, in Hemingway's *A Farewell to Arms*, the well-known opposition of *snow* versus *rain* defines the two domains of the romance. The peaceful snow is clean and quiet; but, when winter ends and the snow turns to rain, hostilities begin to intensify again at the front lines. Frederic Henry must return to the waste land at the front line of the Italian battlefields of World War I, even though Catherine Barkley is afraid of the rain. The rain creates the sea of mud during the retreat from Caporetto, where Italians are shooting their own men. Rain versus snow separates the two domains of love versus death, eros versus thanatos, fertility versus fatality, so that the hero leaves his pregnant beloved and travels over the threshold to the perilous front to prove his honor.

The two domains in the landscape of Romance provide the arena for a physical journey. The protagonist goes in quest across a threshold, often some body of water, separating the two domains. In the perilous domain the hero encounters tests, often in a triad, which give him the opportunity to define his heroic virtue, to show what kind of a hero he is. Does the hero stand out for physical, mental, or moral virtue? Or is the hero perhaps an anti-hero with no pre-eminence or particular virtue? The tests in the perilous domain will show where the hero's virtue resides.

The journey motif carries the hero from one encounter to the next, from one test to another. At the beginning of the journey in the home domain, the hero is well integrated socially with a family, friends, companions, a place in society, and possessions. As he goes deeper and deeper into the perilous domain, all these aids typically are stripped away until, naked and alone, he must confront his ultimate test. At the hero's final encounter, then, he has moved from his comfortable social place to extreme alienation. He has become a stranger in a strange land.

The protagonist faces his ultimate test alone and unaided. If he can not overcome the final test, the pattern of the plot is falling or tragic, and the hero is lost, never to return to his home domain. If he overcomes the ultimate encounter, he reverses the direction of his journey and fights his way back over the threshold to his home domain, in a rising pattern. The Quest thus combines the tragic and the comic, the falling and the rising, motions of the plot into the two halves of the complete perilous journey or Romance.

Once returned to the home domain, the hero finds that his former associates do not understand what he has encountered alone in the perilous domain, so that he is called on to tell his tale to those who have never experienced such terrors personally. In this way a community is re-established between the story teller and his audience and he becomes re-integrated into his home domain, alleviating the alienation he experienced in his dark and lonely ultimate encounter. Such a quest pattern often is mental as well as physical.

The mental quest and the physical quest are frequently superimposed in a single story and they share many common features. In the mental quest the perilous domain is often the subconscious or the unknown. The quest involves crossing the threshold from conscious to dream world, searching scarcely remembered mental fragments for a hidden meaning. Freudian analysis of dreams is an example of the internalization of the quest pattern. The common observation that Conrad's "Heart of Darkness" is an external journey physically into the Dark Continent of Africa, but at the same time an internal exploration of the darkness of the human heart, reveals how the pattern of mental quest coincides with that of a physical quest in Conrad's text. Conrad's *Heart of Darkness* and *Lord Jim*, Charlotte Brontë's *Jane Eyre*, Ford's Tietjens Tetralogy, Rhys's *Wide Sargasso Sea*, as well as Ernest Hemingway's *A Farewell to Arms*, all resemble the family of quest stories in their fictional landscape, opposed domains, journey motif, and episodes testing the protagonist's heroic virtue.

Hemingway, who was Ford Madox Ford's assistant editor in 1924 on *The Transatlantic Review* and whose early fiction appeared there in its "Work in Progress" section, tends to employ the quest pattern uncritically in *A Farewell to Arms*, whereas Conrad in *Heart of Darkness* and Rhys in *Wide Sargasso Sea* force the form of the quest to evolve and transform itself. Conrad and Rhys internalize the quest by mounting onto the external spectacle of a physical journey, the internal, psychological journey of a story teller into his or her own perilous memories and thoughts. Physically, Marlow goes up the Congo River in quest of Kurtz. Psychologically, Marlow on the deck of the Nellie crosses the mental threshold into his dark memories in quest of truth.

The reader, for his or her part, also crosses a threshold when entering the perilous domain of the text, the weird land of fiction. Like Marlow the protagonist and Marlow the story teller entering their unknown territories, the reader who crosses the threshold into the text loses touch with the comfortable land marks and orientation of his or her homeland's parochial attitudes. In this way, the audience re-enacts in its process of reading a major element in the structure of the text. The fictional protagonist is tested to see if he overpowers, outwits, or morally overwhelms his oppositions by his virtue. The heroic story teller unflinchingly exposes memories, delusions, and dreams to see what they mean. The heroic reader does battle with the text to resolve its enigmas and solve its puzzles.

The protagonist may go on a physical journey into the perilous domain, as the agent Marlow travels into darkest Africa upriver seeking Kurtz; but, additionally, the story teller Marlow goes on a mental journey into his memories on a quest to tell his tale. The reader, too, enters the perilous domain of the text where heroic virtues are required to emerge and to give an account of the terror and alienation at its center. It takes great courage to see what is at the dark heart of a story and perhaps even greater courage sometimes to see what is *not* at its heart. What if the story is hollow at its core, no kernel inside the shell of words? What if fiction finally has no answer to real human problems, leaving the reader of a text like Wallace Stevens's "The Snow Man,"

> . . . who listens in the snow,
> And, nothing himself, beholds
> Nothing that is not there and the nothing that is.

What if the very ideas of fidelity, honor, and heroism are bogus, so that the death of Kurtz is no different from the death of Lord Jim?

Traditionally, the story of the heroic quest is an instrument to teach a tribe's warlike youth their tradition of honor, to provide a code of conduct. Fictional narratives like *Heart of Darkness* and *Lord Jim*, however, force a restructuring of the tradition of the romance quest, turning the quest pattern inward and making it critical of the notion of honor itself. These texts question how an impression of heroism is established and maintained. Lord Jim is depicted in the opening paragraphs of the text as addicted to reading about heroic adventures in the "sea life of light literature" (LJ 5.09). Ironically, he is reading *about* such adventures when his first opportunity to play the true hero occurs. A storm at sea and a shipwreck in the harbor give the cadets of his officers' training ship a chance to man the life boat, but Jim is reading *about* heroics and is too late jumping to his rightful station rowing stroke in the cutter. So, he jumps too late toward the role of hero fortuitously open to him and he misses his chance. This episode displays Conrad's customary distrust of the imagination as a guide to day-to-day conduct. After all, Conrad's father's romantic notions of revolutionary heroism led him into an association with the Polish revolution whose consequences were extremely painful not only for Conrad's father, but for his entire family, including the author Conrad himself. Being a hero in the real world seldom resembles what imaginative literature suggests.

Fate apparently has marked Jim to be the butt of a cruel joke. Having jumped too late for the cutter to become a hero on his training ship, he resolves to "jump smart" in the future. This mechanical formula, however, proves his undoing in the Patna episode, his second test. As Marlow observes, the plot of *Lord Jim* unrolls as if some infernal powers had selected Jim "for the victim of their practical joke" (LJ 131.12). The frequency of occurrence in the text of *Lord Jim* of the class of words like "joke" (11 instances), "joker" (1), "jokes" (3), "joking" (2), "jokingly" (1), "jocular" (1), suggests that the concept so denominated is resonant.

Often the plots of Conrad's tales can be compressed into the format of a joke comprised of a set-up followed by a punchline. *Lord Jim*'s central episode, the abandonment of the Patna, might be seen like a circus clown's routine in which an enormous flurry of activity builds an expectation of some terrific coming event, but nothing much happens. Imagine a gang of clowns rushing about preparing an enormous cannon to fire. After incredibly energetic preparations, the cannon finally goes off with a little *poof* and a tiny wisp of smoke. So Jim in terror on the deck of the Patna with the storm bearing down on him, the bulkhead ready to split below the water line, the crowd of Pilgrims set to panic and riot, the fellow officer at Jim's feet dead of a heart attack, the lifeboat stuck, and his commanding officer shouting illegal orders, jumps. The following anticlimax punchline might be, "and the Patna didn't even sink."

Ford's *The Good Soldier* and his Tietjens Tetralogy sometimes called "Parade's End," composed of *Some Do Not* (1924), *No More Parades* (1925), *A Man Could Stand Up* (1926), and *The Last Post* (1928), are filled with funny scenes: gallows humor, grotesque revelations, laughable loves, anticlimaxes, verbal wit. Almost every page moves the reader to laughter. Yet the overall effect of reading these novels is far from a fun-filled romp. Why are readers reluctant to admit that these texts embody the ridiculous to a high degree? What sets up the tension in them between the ridiculous and the tragic?

Mark Schorer in his "Interpretation" introductory to the 1957 Vintage Press reprint of *The Good Soldier*, which initiated the revival of Ford's modern reputation as a writer, asserts that the text is a "comedy of humor" with "wonderfully comic events—little Mrs. Maidan dead in a trunk with her feet sticking out, as though a crocodile had caught her in its giant jaws" (xiv). In such a scene, the laughter in the text flows from the eccentric intelligence of the narrator. Neither Mrs. Maidan's corpse nor a crocodile is funny in isolation, but the collage effect, the incongruous comparison between the trunk containing the dead woman and a reptile devouring its prey, provides a startling juxtaposition when made in the mind of the narrator, so moving the reader to laughter. The surprising association in the observing mind is outlandish. Most readers, however, temper their laughter at this bizarre image with slightly queasy feelings of guilt. One really ought not to compare the poor dead girl to a crocodile's dead meat, we think, as we readers hold our set of values separate from those of the eye observing the scene.

In *A Man Could Stand Up*, Christopher Tietjens looks out from his World War I trench at the front line in France to see suspended in the barbed wire of no man's land "three bundles of rags and what appeared to be a very large squashed cow" (PE 552). Tietjens remembers the previous night looking at his fellow officers sitting at mess and wondering which of them would be killed next. He wonders, "How the devil had that fellow managed to get smashed into that shape? It was improbable." The sudden, improbable metamorphosis of a human being into a very large squashed cow or of a dead woman into a crocodile's dinner are funny as mental events, as forbidden comparisons made deep in the mind. Normally such things are better left unexpressed, or relegated to the dream world of secret, nightmare vision.

Next to the grotesque squashed cow in the barbed wire, Tietjens sees suspended another

> Melodramatic object, the head cast back to the sky. One arm raised in the
> attitude of, say, a Walter Scott Highland officer waving his men on. Waving
> a sword that wasn't there . . . That was what the wire did for you. Supported
> you in grotesque attitudes, even in death. (552)

In this single surreal image of no man's land, appear the main techniques
of Ford's grim comedy: sudden incongruous comparisons and juxtapositions,
grotesque frozen attitudes, and deformed stereotypes.

The Tietjens Tetralogy records an apocalyptic breaking of nations in the years
of World War I. It resembles other large-scale portraits of periods of wide social
and political change like, for example, Leo Tolstoy's (1828-1910) *War and
Peace* (1864-69) set in the period from approximately 1805 to 1820, covering
the invasion of Russia by Napoleon and the changes caused in every aspect of
Russian life by this catastrophe. In its wide historical background, the Tietjens
Tetralogy gives the reader a panorama of violent dislocation on a scale similar
to Tolstoy's.

The Tietjens Tetralogy shows a family resemblance to many historical
romances, including Tolstoy's *War and Peace*, in which an enormous turning
point in world history becomes the setting or background for small-scale
individual passion. Margaret Mitchell's (1900-49) *Gone With the Wind* (1936)
provides a well-known example of such a story, which uses the large screen of the
destruction of the Confederacy in the American Civil War and the Reconstruction
of the American South for its setting, while the focus of attention is on an
intimate erotic foursome. The effect of framing a love affair by the fate of
nations is to infuse the erotic theme with grand importance, so that the flames of
all Atlanta burning add heat to the merely human passion. Jules Roy's epic
treatment of the French colonial experience, *Les Chevaux du Soleil* (1980),
likewise depicts vast changes socially, economically, and politically in North
Africa from the initial French incursion until the withdrawal of the French forces
three generations later. Like Mitchell, Roy uses the broad historical events as a
stage for the passionate interplay of a few central characters.

In Ford's Tietjens Tetralogy, as in the panoramas of Tolstoy, Mitchell, and
Roy, the historical movement is vast and irresistible. The background proclaims
the reign of *Mutability* and the *Vanity of Human Wishes*. Every detail of human
life is shifting. Nothing is permanent. Death and destruction dominate the
entire scene. The overall direction of the plot in such historical romances
is falling, displaying the inevitability of thanatos and loss. Against this grim
background there springs the feeble opposition of eros, love and hope for the
future generations. The juxtaposition of the vast destructive forces of indifferent
nature renders poignant the eternal longing of lover for beloved to create a cozy
place, a safe haven from the storm outside.

Such historical romances center on a few erotically connected characters so that the vast, generally falling, motion of the plot opposes the intimate personal feelings of the central characters. The laughter in the text is defiant in the face of death. The intimate, domestic, erotic, and comic is embedded in a larger framework of the impersonal, cosmic, thanatic, and tragic.

Conrad's *The Shadow Line*, which was serialized in Ford's *The English Review* (September 1916—March 1917), describes the defiant laughter of the mate Burns in the face of threatening impersonal natural forces. On his becalmed ship, Mr. Burns imagines the utter hopelessness of their situation, "He screamed piercingly and burst into such a loud laugh as I had never heard before. It was a provoking, mocking peal, with a hair-raising, screeching over-note of defiance" (176.22-24). Mr. Burns's mad, uncanny laughter apparently causes the winds to blow and the ship, like the bark of the Ancient Mariner in Coleridge's poem, to move forward once again. Written at the outset of World War I and dedicated to his son Borys and all the younger generation who bore the brunt of combat, *The Shadow Line* illustrates Conrad's formulaic use of laughter to defy impersonal, overwhelming natural forces.

Both Ford's *The Good Soldier* and his Tietjens Tetralogy follow the program of Mr. Burns in Conrad's *The Shadow Line*, to laugh in the teeth of destruction. In *The Good Soldier* the protagonist, Edward Ashburnham, is humiliated and reduced to suicide. The perfect ideal of knighthood is destroyed, shown to be merely a dream. Chivalry is dead in the modern world. As Ford in *The March of Literature from Confucius to Modern Times* asserts, Cervantes (1547-1616) destroyed the ideal of chivalry when he exposed his Don Quixote to the impoverished rascality of contemporary Spain. The juxtaposition of the crazy idealism of Don Quixote with the practical realism of Sancho Panza creates a doubled foil, a pair of characters like Dowell and Ashburnham or Marlow and Lord Jim. In *The Good Soldier* Ford reconsiders the argument of Cervantes and retraces the destruction of his chivalric knight who is so hopelessly out of place in the modern world.

The Quixotic Edward Ashburnham is destroyed, his virtues steamrolled out by dominant mediocrity, but the final word in *The Good Soldier*, after all the blood and furor, is uttered by the mad woman, Nancy Rufford. In the concluding pages of the text, Dowell imagines Edward Ashburnham, dead like some fabulous hero, "I seem to see poor Edward, naked and reclining amidst darkness, upon cold rocks, like one of the ancient Greek damned, in Tartarus or wherever it was" (GS 286.16-18). At that point in the text Dowell remembers that the grief-crazed girl, Nancy, like some prophetic Sibyl, rendered her mad judgment of events by repeating the single formulaic word, "shuttlecocks." Dowell speculates that perhaps she is thinking that she is like a shuttlecock, tossed between powerful personalities, or that we all are like shuttlecocks knocked about by forces outside our control. Typically, Dowell's explanations seem obtuse, to be too feeble for the circumstance. Insane Nancy utters an apparently inappropriate word, like Mr. Burns laughing at the hopeless calm. The reader hesitates, hearing "shuttlecocks," between laughter and despair, on the uneasy edge of a joke gone wrong. Such ambivalent laughter is characteristic of Ford's texts.

Consider the totally daft situation Ford develops early in *Some Do Not . . .* at Mrs. Duchemin's breakfast party (PE page 95 and following). Christopher Tietjens's unscrupulous friend, Macmaster, is writing a book on Dante Gabriel Rossetti. Macmaster needs to consult the Reverend Mr. Duchemin, who is an authority on the Pre-Raphaelite poets, on a detail about one of Rossetti's female models. Macmaster finds Mrs. Duchemin very sympathetic and secures from her an invitation for Tietjens and himself to her elegant breakfast party. At this party, Macmaster and Mrs. Duchemin rapidly warm to each other and end up kissing, in a prelude to their future illicit love affair. At the same party, Tietjens sees Valentine Wannop helping serve the dishes and begins to consider her as his possible mistress, once his troubled marriage with his wife, Sylvia, is straightened out. The scene, therefore, is like a Restoration comedy in that two pairs of illicit lovers are struggling to come together secretly within the restrictive impediments of polite, decent behavior. One pair of lovers, the Macmaster-Mrs. Duchemin couple, is more forward and considerably cruder than the other. So as dishes are served and polite conversation is maintained, overheated hands touch, glances are exchanged, even an astonishing kiss takes place. The polite veneer covers, barely, a sexual jungle. The gentle reader, aghast, laughs uneasily at such very bad behavior.

To this louche breakfast party comes the wronged husband, the Anglican minister wearing his clerical collar, Mr. Duchemin, who is physically a handsome specimen, but mentally unbalanced. Lost in his recollections of the history of Dante Gabriel Rossetti's troubled affairs, he does not notice his own wife's randy behavior. He is remarkably absentminded or obtuse.

The Reverend Mr. Duchemin is accompanied by Parry, a burly ex-prizefighter, and it soon appears that Mr. Duchemin is quite insane, given to shouting out obscene statements, with little or no provocation, in the midst of his learned literary disquisitions. His obscenities humiliate his wife, who tries desperately to manage him so that they go unnoticed. When there is no other recourse, Parry's job is to get Mr. Duchemin out of the room. In this way the fragile etiquette of an elegant English breakfast party can prevail. Not only are Tietjens and Macmaster both gradually warming to their future mistresses in this scene, they are both gradually coming to realize that the Reverend Mr. Duchemin is crazy.

The nightmarish scene comes to its climax when Mr. Duchemin is in the process of telling an obscene anecdote. Macmaster asks Mrs. Duchemin,

"I can stop him, shall I?"

She said: "Yes! Yes! Anything!" He observed tears; isolated upon her cheeks, a thing he had never seen. With caution and with hot rage he whispered into the prize-fighter's hairy ear that was held down to him:

"Punch him in the kidney. With your thumb. As *hard* as you can without breaking your thumb . . ."

Mr. Duchemin had just declaimed: "I, too, after my nuptials . . ."

He began to wave his arms, pausing and looking from unlistening face to unlistening face. Mrs. Duchemin had just screamed.

Mr. Duchemin thought that the arrow of God struck him. He imagined himself an unworthy messenger. In such pain as he had never conceived of he fell into his chair and sat huddled up, a darkness covering his eyes.

"He won't get up again." Macmaster whispered to the appreciative pugilist. "He'll want to. But he'll be afraid."

He said to Mrs. Duchemin: "Dearest Lady! It's all over. I assure you of that. It's a scientific nerve counter-irritant." (PE 100)

At this point Mrs. Duchemin and Macmaster begin to hold hands, cementing their sexual attraction, while the breakfast party continues with polite non-sequitur conversation as though nothing at all strange or unusual had happened.

Here amidst the tinkle of fine china and polite murmuring in a country parsonage, Ford has imagined a scene as wacky as anything in the fiction of Robert Coover, John Barth, or Thomas Pynchon. Ford is able to enclose the mental incoherence of Mr. and Mrs. Duchemin in a frame of orderly gentility. Later in the novel, Ford reverses that formula at the front lines of World War I, where it is the frame of trench warfare that is incoherent and the individuals caught in that environment who struggle to maintain some vestige of mental coherence, for example by writing Latin poetry during a barrage.

It is useful to make a distinction between subversive versus corrective laughter. For example in Henry Fielding's (1707-1754) "Preface" to *Joseph Andrews* (1742), laughter is defined as socially corrective. Fielding asserts that the only true source of the ridiculous is affectation or pretense, that affection arises only from vanity or hypocrisy, and that the exposure or revelation of a vain or of a hypocritical pretense causes laughter when observed. Laughter is therefore an instrument to correct affectation, to teach us not to pretend to be what we are not, to know ourselves truly and to display ourselves strictly as we are. Fielding's theory apparently explains why stock stereotypes like the braggart soldier, the conniving servant, or the religious hypocrite generate laughter when the audience sees through the vanity or hypocrisy of the false face which the character presents to the public.

We laugh when we see the religious hypocrisy of Moliere's (1622-73) Tartuffe revealed. In a similar way, the missionary zeal of Conrad's Kurtz in the "Heart of Darkness" is shown as a vain or hypocritical mask for murderous greed and self-aggrandizement, when the dying Kurtz speaks of

> "My Intended, my ivory, my station, my river, my"——everything belonged to him.

Marlow astutely deflates Kurtz's vanity by observing,

> Everything belonged to him——but that was a trifle. The thing was to know what he belonged to, how many powers of darkness claimed him for their own. (HD 116)

Kurtz in this scene displays the comic trope of *the possessor possessed*. In his vanity Kurtz imagines that he will possess Africa, little knowing that he is himself possessed. Appropriately, Marlow holds his breath in this scene "in expectation of hearing the wilderness burst into a prodigious peal of laughter that would shake the fixed stars in their places" (HD 116).

Such grim, cosmic laughter at the vanity of human wishes echoes throughout the fictions of Ford, Conrad, and Rhys. Presumably, the severed head which sleeps on a pole outside the hut of Kurtz is a party to the joke, "the shrunken dry lips showing a narrow white line of the teeth, was smiling, too, smiling continuously at some endless and jocose dream of that eternal slumber" (HD 130). When we step back from the texts and take a look at their broad patterns, Conrad's or Ford's works often seem to be built on a joke gone wrong. Often they show the vain affectation of man imagining he is in control or that he understands his situation fully, when in fact he lacks control and self-knowledge. Remember Lord Jim, selected by the "powers . . . for the victim of their practical joke" (131.12). The punch line for the joke on Jim is that the Pilgrim ship did not sink, all the fear and turmoil of the craven European officers in the crisis was groundless.

An examination of little Mrs. Maidan dead in the crocodile trunk's jaws, the British officer squashed into a cow in the barbed wire between the trenches, the kidney punch delivered to the obscene Reverend Mr. Duchemin, Kurtz thinking he possesses what is valuable in Africa, or Jim jumping for his life from a non-sinking ship, all display the theory of the ridiculous which Henri Bergson articulated in *Le Rire* (1900). Bergson asks why a jack in the box, or a marionette, or a Punch and Judy show are funny. He suggests that such figures evoke laughter because their behavior is involuntary, resulting from rigidity or momentum, as if a part of a machine. To be truly alive, to enjoy the *elan vital,* requires tension and elasticity in action. The ridiculous character inattentively or absentmindedly abdicates or gives up his or her voluntary, flexible life in such a way as to become like a part under the control of a larger machine, moving from a momentum supplied from afar, in a rigid pattern. The British officer squashed into a cow shape and supported by the wire between the trenches, like a marionette on its wire, is funny for the reasons provided by Bergson. Not only is his grotesque death supported by the wire, but also his death was caused by a tangle of political strings expressed in the mechanism of the military. He was deprived of his personal will and made into a cog in the fighting machine.

The title of Ford's novel, *Parade's End*, of course, refers to the demobilization ceremonies surrounding the Armistice ending World War I. A military *Parade*, however, is particularly effective as a demonstration of Bergson's theory of the ridiculous. Each individual soldier on parade surrenders his personal will to mechanical, predictable movement in response to an external momentum: the grand army, flags waving, buttons shining, drums and trumpets braying, goose stepping off a cliff.

To "forget yourself" and absentmindedly allow your action to be dictated from the outside renders you subject to ridicule. It is laughter that awakens an agent to vital, elastic, voluntary, individual life. Mr. Burns, becalmed, frees himself by laughter. The liberating power of laughter stems from an ability to see through the network of forces restraining the true volition of a character. We laugh at Mrs. Duchemin and Macmaster as they display rising erotic interest in each other, but are held apart by the etiquette of an English formal breakfast party. We laugh when we observe that the restrictions are too feeble to thwart the volition. Our laughter celebrates the subversion of rigid, external control of their authentic volition.

P. G. Wodehouse (1902-1975) wrote nearly a hundred novels in which laughter celebrates the subversion of mechanical social order by the elan of Bertie Wooster and his conniving butler, Jeeves. At all costs the intricate mechanism of polite society must appear to be maintained while the secret, unacceptable desires, often erotic in nature, of Bertie Wooster seek gratification. Once the deception begins, it builds enormously complicated structures hiding the truth in more and more precarious ways, until the trickster is finally revealed. If Mark Schorer can laugh at little Mrs. Maidan dead in her trunk with her feet sticking out as though a crocodile had caught her in its jaws, the reader may be excused for thinking, just for a brief moment, that the whole of Ford's *The Good Soldier* is rather similar to an adventure of Bertie Wooster, a grand decade of deception as the foursome maintain the conventions of polite decency so as to conceal the facts of their adultery and betrayal. In the teeth of that mechanism, Nancy Rufford screams "shuttlecocks," where a sternly disapproving aunt might say "fiddlesticks" to Bertie Wooster.

In fact, large sections of both *The Good Soldier* and the Tietjens Tetralogy resemble the second act of a French farce, perhaps *Un fil à la patte* (1894) or *La Pouce à l'oreille* (1907) by Georges Feydeau (1862-1921). Driven by a desire to appear socially correct while gratifying some low desire, Feydeau's characters generally build complex schemes of deception which get out of hand and begin to grow to baroque elaboration. On stage, scene after scene involves mistaken identity, taking "this for that." For example, the husband returning home unexpectedly finds the lover's hat in his wife's bedroom. She tells her husband that the strange hat is a surprise gift she was preparing for him. The husband, pleased with his wife's supposed gift, wears the lover's hat to his club, where he encounters the lover wearing one of the husband's own hats, since the husband has taken the lover's hat. The husband remarks that the lover is wearing a hat identical to one the husband has at home in his closet. And so the deception must build, on and on, until the whole house of cards comes crashing down.

A common trope of the French farce is the scene in the hotel corridor. In a darkened hallway, a row of doors leads presumably to the quarters of the wife, the husband, the lover, the maid, the hotel keeper, *et al.* The farce scarcely needs describing: With a knowing leer aside to the audience, the lover tiptoes out of his room into the door of the wife's bedroom. The husband strolls in and pounds on the wife's door. She opens and distracts him in the hallway as the lover, now disguised as the maid, tries to slip out of the wife's room unnoticed. But the hotel keeper's door pops open and he furiously orders the maid to make up the bed in the husband's room. The husband returns to his room and makes lascivious advances to the maid in disguise. And so on.

Consider Part II of *No More Parades* as a strange mutation of such a French farce. Christopher Tietjens and his bitch-goddess wife, Sylvia, are engaged in a bitter dispute about their divorce. Christopher has been terribly strafed in the filthy, muddy trenches of the front lines of World War I in France. Meanwhile, just a few miles behind the lines, impeccably dressed, elegant and cool, Sylvia is being propositioned by Major Perowne:

> In the admirably appointed, white-enamelled, wickerworked, be-mirrored lounge of the best hotel in town Sylvia Tietjens sat in a wickerwork chair, not listening rather abstractedly to a staff-major who was lachrymosely and continuously begging her to leave her bedroom door unlocked that night. She said:
> 'I don't know . . . Yes, perhaps . . . I don't know . . . ' And looked distantly into a bluish wall-mirror that, like all the rest, was framed with white painted cork bark. She stiffened a little and said:
> 'There's Christopher.'
> The staff major dropped his hat, his stick, and his gloves. (PE 379)

Major Perowne begins to sweat profusely at the sight of the wronged husband in the hotel mirror. As well he might, for in a parody of a government report in Part I of *No More Parades* Christopher Tietjens has given the reader a summary of his situation as he sees it. The main items leading up to the encounter of Christopher Tietjens with Perowne in the hotel are: Sylvia, while pregnant by a man named Drake, tricked Christopher into marrying her. The son of that marriage, who is not the biological offspring of Christopher, is so dear to Christopher that he will not sue Sylvia for a divorce, although she has been unfaithful to him many times. Sylvia, being Roman Catholic and enjoying the economic and social advantages of being Christopher's wife, will not divorce him. Through the son's godfather, General Lord Edward Campion, Sylvia meets Campion's inefficient, but decorative, staff officer, Major Perowne. Perowne and Sylvia secretly live together for several months. During that time Christopher met and fell in love with Valentine Wannop. They agreed to sleep together, but the events of war intervened and Christopher "merely touched the brim of my cap and said: *So long!*" (PE 245-47). Now, Sylvia has come with Perowne to France to consolidate her position as Christopher's wife and as mother of the heir to his Yorkshire estate, Groby.

Although Sylvia tells Perowne, "You can come . . . I won't lock my door. But I don't say that you'll get anything . . . or that you'll like what you get" (PE 387), she later agrees to discuss their marriage problems with her husband Christopher in that same room at that same time.

Sylvia and Christopher are dancing in the midst of an air raid in the hotel bar when he asks her to talk seriously about their relationship. She replies, "in my room, then! I'm dog tired . . . I haven't slept for six nights . . . In spite of drugs" (PE 443). Christopher follows her up the stairs looking at "her gown of gold tissue . . . As they mounted the stairs she thought what a fat tenor Tannhäuser always was! . . . The Venusberg music dinning in her ears" (PE 443). At this point, a time shift interrupts the narrative. We flash forward a few days and learn that Christopher is now under military arrest for striking his superior officer, Perowne. The upshot of this misadventure is that General Campion reassigns Christopher to the front lines and almost certain death, so as to avoid a public scandal. Of course, if Christopher were killed in battle, Sylvia and her son would inherit the Tietjens estate.

What happened in the darkened hotel corridor? In Part III of *No More Parades* the fatigued and battle-stressed Tietjens associates a metal container of smelling salts, which he sees, with the brass handle of the door of Sylvia's hotel room. In a wild mental collage, mixing remembrance, fantasy, and present events, Tietjens recalls the door handle of Sylvia's room moving almost imperceptibly. By association of ideas, perhaps falsifying the events so as to protect Sylvia's reputation, Tietjens tells the investigating officer that Major Perowne and a military police officer broke into his wife's room while she was undressed with him. They were drunk and he threw them out, Tietjens says. They, too, claim to have made a drunken blunder. No matter how painful, Tietjens will keep up appearances. His story is that his wife is blameless. Perowne was drunk. Tietjens hit Perowne as a result of a misunderstanding. Tietjens says, "The thing is to be able to stick to the integrity of your character, whatever earthquake sets the house tumbling over your head" (PE 454). Maintaining appearances, protecting Sylvia's reputation, in this case causes Tietjens to be sent "up the line . . . That's certain death" (PE 476).

The reader knows that Sylvia lured Perowne and Tietjens to their confrontation in her room. She stands to profit by Tietjens's death. Like a fat tenor playing Tannhäuser, Tietjens enters his Venusberg captivated, manipulated, forgetful of himself. It is a comedy with nobody laughing.

# CHAPTER VI
## THE OCULAR TROPE

*The ocular trope. Cognitive dissonance and turbulence in denominating the visual. Is reading a text like seeing an object? Naive realism. Communal agreement. Alienation versus community of values. The artist's eye.*

In William Shakespeare's *Othello* (III, iii), Othello demands that Iago provide "the ocular proof" that his wife, Desdemona, is unfaithful. For Othello, seeing is believing. Iago soon shows the magic handkerchief, once given by Othello as a pledge of love to Desdemona, in the hands of Cassio, her alleged lover. Satisfied that he now has seen proof of her infidelity, Othello proceeds to kill her. But, of course, the evidence is misleading. Othello's eyes deceive him. His perception that his gift handkerchief is in Cassio's hands is correct, but the inference he draws from that perception is false. The handkerchief in Cassio's hand presents Othello with a problem in pseudo-speciation. Is Desdemona his loving and faithful wife or has she shifted her allegiance to more libertine behavior alleged by Iago to be characteristic of the Venetian court. To what group does the white woman belong: faithful wife, or unfaithful courtesan? As an indication of her pseudo-speciation, how does Othello understand her misplaced handkerchief? The real audience reading or hearing the play knows that Othello's interpretation of what he sees is mistaken.

Earlier in the same scene, Othello cites as evidence that Desdemona truly loves him that "she had eyes and chose me." Desdemona's eyes, too, mislead her, for in leaving her father's house to follow Othello, she chooses death, mistakenly trusting in Othello's wisdom and kindness. Appearances can be deceptive. When Othello learns at the tragic conclusion of the play that his eyes have led him astray, that Desdemona's infidelity is nothing but his delusion, he kills himself. The dramatization of the events in the play *Othello* exploits the difference between the chronology of understanding of the real audience versus that of Othello. The audience sees the handkerchief in Cassio's hand and thinks that Iago has planted it there, whereas at the same time Othello sees it and thinks that Desdemona has betrayed him. Othello's understanding is out of synchrony with the understanding of the real audience. Sometimes we say that such a situation displays "dramatic irony." The audience understands something in a radically different way from the understanding of a limited character on stage. At the end of the play, when Othello's understanding coincides with that of the audience, narrative closure occurs. The play ends when the audience and the characters on stage reach a communal agreement.

In Classical Greek the single verb, *eido*, bears the double meaning of *to see* and *to know*. It is possible to read the story of Oedipus the Tyrant, told by Sophocles, as an extended exploration of these two separate branches of signification at war in this single word, *eido*. It might even be argued that the name of King Oedipus, usually linked etymologically with Greek words meaning something like "wounded foot," actually is related more nearly to forms of the verb *eido*. Onomastically, perhaps, King Oedipus is "someone who has seen and knows" (Oid' hopos). When Oedipus has eyes to see, he mistakenly thinks he knows; but blinded, he truly understands. Here we must pause and examine the word "truly," in the preceding sentence. Does "truly" mean anything more than a communal agreement between the characters on stage and the audience as to what is happening? The closure of the drama occurs when the audience and agents agree as to what they see.

At the center of the impressionist movement in art and literature there is a contradiction embedded in the language itself hovering about the trope "to see." Charlotte's Brontë's blinding of Rochester in Thornfield Hall ablaze becomes the link connecting her text to *Wide Sargasso Sea*. Rhys depicts young Rochester, disgusted with his bride, Antoinette, and sickened by Christophine's love potion, confronting the obeah:

> "I would give my eyes never to have seen this abominable place."
> She laughed. "And that's the first damn word of truth you speak. You choose
> what you give, eh? Then you choose. You meddle in something and perhaps
> you don't know what it is." She began to mutter to herself. (161)

This grim joke at the heart of Rhys's *Wide Sargasso Sea* belongs to the class of folk tales cautioning "be careful what you wish for." Rochester cannot understand what Christophine is saying and he cannot even recognize what language she is muttering. It is likely that in this scene she invokes a voodoo curse in incomprehensible words, which reaches fulfillment years later in England when Rochester's home goes up in flames taking with it his eyesight. Like Othello's handkerchief, there is magic in the web of this scene which connects the catastrophic conclusion of *Jane Eyre* to previous events in Antoinette Cosway's home domain.

The reader of Conrad, Ford, and Rhys will sense that something is "going on" in many of their texts with the group of words related to *eyes, seeing, sight; mirror, reflection, impression*. Such words signify a turbulent arena, an area of conflict in the text. On the one hand, when Ford entitles *Part III* of *Joseph Conrad: A Personal Remembrance*, "It is above all to make you see," he seems to be endorsing a naive empiricism. When Ford asserts that Conrad's "chief message to mankind is set at the head of this chapter" (JC 168), he seems to be saying that language should be a transparent medium, conveying knowledge of an exterior world with no distortion or interpretation by the author. Convincing fiction should be a plain, unvarnished tale. Yet, on the other hand, the main thrust of the impressionist movement in literature is to challenge the naive realist's visual metaphor. Rhys extends the exploration of the optical trope begun by Conrad and Ford.

Neither Conrad, nor Ford, nor Rhys were systematic, well-trained philosophic thinkers. Nevertheless, their concern with point of view, unreliability, delayed decoding, and their denomination of vocabulary related to reflection, impression, and sight, highlights a central philosophic problem in the modernist revolution: Is reading a text like seeing an object? What actually happens when we form an impression of something outside ourselves? Rhys carries forward the debate against naive realism begun by Conrad and Ford, particularly in her patterns of imagery and in the limited narrators' situation in *Wide Sargasso Sea*. Like Helmholtz observing that sound must be divided into *sensation* and *conception* and that the *conception* is to a large degree constructed by the receptive mind, Rhys sees language as a stimulus for the creation of the readers' conceptions.

When Conrad, Ford, and Rhys develop eccentric and unreliable narrative point of view, delayed decoding of turbulent signifiers, dramatic irony, and open ambiguities in plot, ideology, and vocabulary, they challenge the notion that language is an adequate model to capture immediate sensation, particularly visual sensation. All three authors explore the decay of the naive realist's belief that language is a transparent medium through which we can see the world as it truly is.

The text of Conrad's "Heart of Darkness" is filled with eyes. "Eyes" occurs forty-nine times, with more than ten additional uses of "eye" in its various forms and compounds. Relative frequency is a tricky concept; but, considering that "tongue" occurs only once and "ears" only six times in the same text, perhaps the reader may suspect that the organ of sight hovers persistently on the edge of Conrad's consciousness as he writes, rather like the great eyes dominating Odilon Redon's (1840-1916) group of paintings and drawings like *Eye-balloon* (1878), *Guardian Spirit of the Waters* (1878), or *The Cyclops* (c. 1914).

Although such distinctions are always a bit fuzzy, it appears that the references to eyes in "Heart of Darkness" can be divided into figurative and literal. Figurative denominations might include the Roman officer invading Great Britain "keeping an eye on a chance of promotion to the fleet at Ravenna" (49); something that happens "under his very eyes" (74); believing or trusting one's own eyes (79, 99); to be as near as if "before my eyes" (81); or to keep one's eyes open (139).

Literal or more concrete signification for "eyes" in "Heart of Darkness" often involves characterization, so that the description of a personage includes his or her eyes, especially as they express the individual's state of mind, for example "his mild, bulging eyes" (70), "cold" eyes (73), and similar cases. More interesting are the eyes of the uncanny women knitting at the gateway of Marlow's adventure, like the Parcae or Norns, who are described "knitting with down-cast eyes" (55), "with unconcerned old eyes" (57). Are these women

prophetic, possessing grim knowledge of the future ahead for those who embark
on the quest into the heart of darkness? Are they like Tiresias, unseeing but gifted
with foresight? Are they uncanny because their eyes are indifferent, watching
the aspiring heroes cross the threshold to be tested in the certain knowledge that
they are doomed? Did these same knitting women see Kurtz pass through that
door on his way to Africa? When Kurtz dies the light is "within a foot of his
eyes" but he thinks he is in darkness (148, 149). When Kurtz's Intended Bride
discusses his fate, her eyes fill with unshed tears (159).

Most frequently, however, Conrad imagines eyes shining from the darkness,
signifying that there is an alien point of view looking Marlow in the face. These
eyes animate the forest, bring the natural landscape alive, and emphasize the
danger of the other. Face to face, eyeball to eyeball, the eyewitness Marlow
sees someone looking back at him from the gloomy depths of the jungle:

> "Suddenly, as though a veil had been removed from my eyes, I made out, deep
> in the tangled gloom, naked breasts, arms, legs, glaring eyes . . . " (110)

Sometimes when eyes come alive in the dusky jungle they evoke pity, as in the
grove of death, where the dying blacks cast their eyes on Marlow (66, 70). At
other times, the eye in the darkness produces terror, as in the cannibal fireman's
eye (103), or in the attack on the steamer and the spear thrust that kills the
helmsman (110, 112, 119). Closed eyes often signify death, as the enigmatically
smiling, severed, black head before Kurtz's dwelling has closed eyelids (130),
and in the grove of death eyes flicker shut as the blacks die (66). Too much
sympathy, on the other hand, causes one to avert the eyes, as Marlow must shut
his eyes while drawing the spear out of the torso of the dying helmsman (119)
and closed eyes render one ineffective, as Marlow scolds his foolish companions
for shooting at the blacks "from the hip with their eyes shut" instead of taking
"aim and firing from the shoulder" (121).

A main concern of "Heart of Darkness" is to warn against seeing things from
only one point of view. In the outer frame on the deck of the *Nellie*, the first
speaker praises the might and glory of England, "The seed of commonwealths,
the germs of Empire" (47). His point of view is immediately undercut by
Marlow's intervention which offers an alternative way to see things, "And this
also, said Marlow suddenly, has been one of the dark places on the earth" (48).
All the eyes looking out of the underbrush at Marlow as he voyages into the
interior of the dark continent, in turn, offer the reader an alternative to Marlow's
view. Those eyes seem to beg the reader to look at these events from their
viewpoint, to share their terrible suffering, to see their just complaint against the
European intrusion.

Turbulence hovers not merely about the word "eye" in the vocabulary
denominated in the text, but in the large structural elements in the story, as well,
such as its embedded multiple, unreliable narration and the abrasion between

persona and dramatic audience on the deck of the Nellie, for example the interjection from the audience as Marlow tells his tale, "Try to be civil, Marlow, growled a voice" (93). Marlow is saying things that the director of companies, the accountant, and the lawyer would rather not hear. He makes them open their eyes to things they would rather not see. Perhaps some of the real readers of this story in England at the turn of this century found the tale equally abrasive or offensive. So, there is a conflict between two different ways of seeing the affair.

The overall design of "Heart of Darkness" might be described as a "mirroring." In past time Marlow had an immediate and painful experience of Africa which he registers mainly in visual scenes. He usually remembers events he witnessed and how things appeared to him. In the fictive present time on the deck of the Nellie, he attempts to translate these remembered visual experiences into language so that his audience of the Director of Companies, the lawyer, the accountant, and the outer narrator can share his outlook. "To see" becomes "to tell" in order to make others "see." In the dark jungle of Africa in previous times, Marlow occasionally saw shining eyes which returned his looks. Likewise, as darkness falls on the deck of the Nellie on the Thames estuary in the fictive present time, the eyes of his audience confront Marlow as he tells his tale. The symmetry of an object confronting its mirror image is reiterated in the systole and diastole of the tide turning in the Thames estuary as the Nellie rests at anchor while Marlow tells his tale and also by the journey motif of the quest as the hero leaves Europe and penetrates to the innermost point on the Congo River only to turn around and retrace his journey, back to his home domain.

Like Othello's ocular proof, Marlow's tale displays deception as he falsely tells the Intended Bride that Kurtz's last words were of her. Perhaps Marlow cannot bear to look directly at her pain, so he averts his eyes as he did when he pulled the spear from his dying Helmsman. Like firing a rifle with eyes shut, averting the eyes is an ineffective and self-defeating way to confront reality, however, as the practical men of business on the deck of the Nellie and the real reader probably would agree.

In Ford's *The Good Soldier*, the group of words composed of "eye," "eyes," and compounds like "eye-openers," accounts for over a hundred tokens occurring in the text. The narrative situation, in which Dowell has seen something in the past and now in the fictive present time tells us about his experience, is like that of Marlow telling his tale on the deck of the Nellie in "Heart of Darkness." Naturally, the rather frequent denomination of the word "eye" in *The Good Soldier* as the site of visual impressions reinforces the overall structure of limited narration in the text: Dowell first sees, then tells what he has seen. Dowell inverts the situation of Othello, in that Dowell's wife indeed *is* a whore—unless Dowell is suffering from hallucinations. Dowell and Marlow both operate by "show and tell," or "see first and tell later." Both hold the readers' interest because deception, delusion, and hallucination may differentiate the speaker's judgment from that of his audience, creating dramatic irony.

The uses of the word "eyes" in Ford's *The Good Soldier* resemble closely Conrad's practice in "Heart of Darkness." The figurative meanings designated in Ford's text appear to include the following: something obvious is "under the eyes" (44.23, 104.13); one flirts by "making eyes at" (210.23, 215.22-23, 215.26); one pays close attention by keeping one's eyes on something (216.05); when one discovers suddenly, one opens one's eyes (235.15); and one's opinion is how it appears in one's eyes, or estimation (277.01). The truth is seen by the eyes of God (282.18).

The range of literal meanings for the keyword "eye" in *The Good Soldier* is not large. In most cases Ford refers to eyes when he wishes to describe character. As a method of characterization, denomination of "eyes" is a handy tool for the novelist, since the eyes often indicate some temporary state of mind or habitual attitude. For example, Edward Ashburnham is introduced to us with "such honest blue eyes, such a touch of stupidity" (9.03). Similar usage, attaching a state of mind, quality, or feeling to a personage abound in the story (14.09, 25.11, 30.11, 31.10, 31.30-31, 32.01, 32.16, 32.28, 35.26, 36.06, 51.09, 54.17, 89.03, 98.16, 99.19, 114.01, 126.17, 133.29, 142.02, 143.06, 146.24, and so on). As the story reaches its fatal conclusion, the reader sees the catastrophe in the mad eyes of Nancy Rufford (288.11) and Edward Ashburnham looks at Dowell with soft and "almost affectionate" eyes just before his suicide (290.05, 290.11).

Over and above simple characterization and indication of mood and attitude, meeting of the eyes can communicate guilty secrets, as mothers teach daughters "with the eyes, or with heart whispering to heart" or lying eyes which can deceive (10.15, 50.19, 151.08), or the eyes provide the path for seduction (49.17). The eye is not merely vulnerable emotionally. It can suffer dangerous wounds of many kinds (103.22, 114.22, 271.03, 282.19). In a few cases, the eye appears as a tool of the intellect, screening information so that the brain asks and the eyes answer, as when someone evaluates a race horse or a person (36.13-17, 37.03). Finally, Ford uses a foreign expression, the common German idiom meaning "a couple alone," translated literally as "under four eyes" (29.17, 59.12), probably to emphasize the German setting of Bad Nauheim and to defamiliarize his language.

One passage featuring the word "eyes" in *The Good Soldier* stands out, however, engaging the reader's authentic interest above all other contexts in which the word occurs. According to Dowell, the eye is the source of erotic desire because the lover wants to invade the beloved's mind and see the world through the beloved's point of view:

> A love affair, a love for any definite woman—is something in the nature of a widening of the experience . . . a broadening of the outlook, or . . . an

acquiring of new territory. A turn of the eye-brow, a tone of the voice, a queer characteristic gesture— . . . cause to arise the passion of love—all these things are like so many objects on the horizon of the landscape that tempt a man to walk beyond the horizon, to explore. He wants to get . . . behind those eye-brows with the peculiar turn, as if he desired to see the world with the eyes that they overshadow . . . It can be aroused by a glance of the eye in passing . . . The soul of a man is the craving for identity with the woman that he loves. He desires to see with the same eyes, to touch with the same sense of touch . . . to lose his identity, to be enveloped . . . We are all so afraid, we are all so alone . . . (130.26-132.06)

This apostrophe to the erotic affair in Ford's *The Good Soldier* looks back to Marlow's quest to penetrate to the interior of Africa and could be read as a gloss, as well, on the conclusion of Charlotte Brontë's *Jane Eyre* where her text links closely to Rhys's *Wide Sargasso Sea*.

It is a commonplace observation that colonial and post-colonial fiction often imagines the occupied territory as female, a body to be dominated, raped, invaded, and violated. Perhaps Ford's idea of a love affair, described in the passage quoted above from *The Good Soldier*, suggests why Conrad is able to imagine his fictional colonial environments restricted to a cast of characters which is almost entirely male. For Conrad the colonized space fills the role of the female. In "Heart of Darkness," the eyes of Africa in the grove of death, hidden in the jungle, or in the cannibal crew, supply an erotic displacement of the feminine. Kurtz and Marlow penetrate and violate Africa in a quest to get "behind those eyebrows," to lose their European identity and be enveloped in Africa, to heal the loneliness and fear of their own alienation.

In *Jane Eyre* St. John Rivers is filled with missionary zeal to convert all India, like Kurtz when first bound for Africa (JE 813.08 and following). When St. John proposes marriage to Jane, she is horrified and scorns his offer. Of course, Jane's rejection of St. John is motivated by her prior affection for Rochester and, although she respects many of St John's good qualities, she does not love him (841.13). The reader probably sympathizes with Jane's rejection of St. John, even though she risks eternal damnation for her illegitimate love for the married Rochester (844.23 and following). When she receives the mysterious cry, "Jane, Jane, Jane," calling her back to Rochester (849.13), few readers will hear it as the voice of the devil leading her astray morally, although plainly St. John Rivers would give it such a diabolic explanation.

Why do we find St. John so unfit as a husband for Jane? Perhaps, in part, St. John has already substituted his missionary zeal and his concomitant drive for colonial domination of conquered territory in place of human love. St. John wants to get into the minds and hearts of India, and there is no place in his scheme for an authentic love affair with Jane. For Jane to marry St. John, she needs to believe something like Marlow's lie to the Intended Bride of Kurtz. It is very unlikely that St. John's dying words will be of Jane. St. John's eyes are on what he thinks is the larger prize, the conversion of India.

Rochester, however, as a youth has visited the colonial sugar plantations of the West Indies, married Antoinette Cosway, and rejected the role of colonizer. Rochester will not step into the shoes of Kurtz, but St. John might. St. John preaches to Jane from the twenty-first chapter of *Revelations* that she is in danger of falling into "the lake which burneth with fire and brimstone" (844.20-21), if she does not marry him and join the missionary cause in India. The twenty-first chapter of *Revelations* describes the vision of the "holy city, new Jerusalem, coming down out of heaven from God, prepared as a bride adorned for her husband." Chapter twenty-one of *Revelations* promises that "he who conquers shall have this heritage, and I will be his God and he shall be my son. But as for the cowardly, the faithless, the polluted . . . their lot shall be in the lake that burns with fire and brimstone."

When Rochester emerges from the fire at Thornfield Hall, which destroys his last link with his colonial past, he calls for his bride, "Jane! Jane! Jane!" (JE 849.13). Now blinded, he sees the light. In the twenty-first chapter of *Revelations*, in the new Jerusalem, there is "no need of sun or moon to shine upon it, for the Glory of God is its light, and its lamp is the Lamb." The dwelling place for Jane as Rochester's bride is similarly lit for him by a spiritual light of love.

The erotic consummation of *Jane Eyre* depends on a struggle to master the eye. In the concluding pages of the novel, Jane expresses so much delight in Rochester's blindness that some male readers might find her attitude a bit sinister or threatening:

> Mr. Rochester continued blind the first two years of our union: perhaps it was that circumstance that drew us so very near—that knit us so very close; for I was then his vision, as I am still his right hand. Literally . . . He saw nature—he saw books through me; and never did I weary of gazing for his behalf, and of putting into words the effect of field, tree, town, river, cloud, sunbeam - of the landscape before us; of the weather round us—and impressing by sound on his ear what light could no longer stamp on his eye." (JE 909.14-25)

Of course, Jane is delighted that Rochester now needs her. She has a useful role to play in serving him. He is bound to her in gratitude. Their separate identities are united in his visual dependence on her. Later, under Jane's careful nursing, he regains a small part of the ability to see, and when their son is born, "the boy inherited his own eyes, as they once were—large, brilliant, and black" (JE 910.27-8). Seeing for Rochester, becoming his eyes, Jane becomes flesh of his flesh. The lovers are intimately yoked together because she enters behind his eyebrows. Jane ends up on top because Rochester is cast in the blindfolded bottom role.

In telling her tale, Jane forces the reader to play the role of Rochester. The reader is blind to the story, until Jane's voice reveals the tale. Only through her voice does the reader see the fictional landscapes and events of the novel, as she puts "into words the effect of field, tree, town, river, cloud, sunbeam," both for the benefit of the reader and of Rochester. The character Jane guides the reader, otherwise blind to her fictional world, by her voice. In Conrad's *Under Western Eyes*, the Teacher of Languages similarly reports the Razumov affair as a "witness of things Russian, unrolling their Eastern logic under my western eyes" (UWE 376.33-34).

It is not surprising that mirrors and other reflecting surfaces figure prominently in impressionist fiction. How else can impressions be formed, if not by reflection. In *Wide Sargasso Sea* as the family estate, Coulibri, burns and a crowd of hostile blacks threaten the terrified child, Antoinette, and her fleeing family, Antoinette sees her black playmate and companion, Tia:

> Then, not so far off, I saw Tia and her mother and I ran to her, for she was all that was left of my life as it had been. We had eaten the same food, slept side by side, bathed in the same river. As I ran, I thought, I will live with Tia and I will be like her . . . I saw the jagged stone in her hand but I did not see her throw it . . . We stared at each other, blood on my face, tears on hers. It was as if I saw myself. Like in a looking-glass. (45)

In fact, Tia hurls the stone and so severely wounds Antoinette that she is confined to bed for many days. She painfully severs her connection with the black girl and never again sees her as her own mirror image.

When Antoinette is imprisoned in England, part of her madness is that she is deprived of her self-image:

> There is no looking-glass here and I don't know what I am like now. I remember watching myself brush my hair and how my eyes looked back at me. The girl I saw was myself yet not quite myself. Long ago when I was a child and very lonely I tried to kiss her. But the glass was between us—hard, cold and misted over with my breath. Now they have taken everything away. What am I doing in this place and who am I? (180)

The mirror sets up a twin or shadow character and the deprivation of that reflection is like the folk motif of the stolen shadow. The detached, missing soul indicates the character's extreme alienation. Antoinette's inner vitality is replaced by an empty, hateful superficiality. The mirror is also, like dreams and stories, the threshold to the domain of the imagination and memory, an escape from the world which is directly present to the senses.

In creating these scenes, Rhys follows the pattern set in the vocabulary of Charlotte Brontë's parent text. In the opening pages of *Jane Eyre*, the child, Jane, is treated cruelly by the Reed family. To escape their nastiness through the power of her imagination, she reads a book. The abusive boy, John Reed, discovers her reading and tells her that she is merely an impoverished dependent and that she has no business reading. He orders her to stand "out of the way of the mirror and the windows" (9.16-17). He then throws the book at her so that she cuts her head and falls. Like Antoinette's wound from the stone thrown by Tia, Jane's injury causes her to become seriously ill from the assault. Later, looking in the mirrors which line the frightening red room where she is confined (JE 16.17), she thinks of the ghost of dead Mr. Reed returning to avenge the oppressed and she is terrified (22.14).

When Jane is about to be married to Rochester, she encounters his mad wife via a mirror. Jane sees the reflection of a strange woman, tall with dark, long hair. This woman puts on Jane's wedding veil and regards herself in a mirror (577.20). Jane sees the woman as fearful, ghastly, discolored, and savage. Later when Jane looks at herself in the mirror in her wedding clothes, she sees "a robed and veiled figure, so unlike my usual self that it seemed almost the image of a stranger" (585.15-16). In the second passage, the mirror functions like the threshold between front and back space which defines a dual character. The front space offers a public role to play, the respectable wife. Hidden in the back space is the private identity of the individual which must be masked so as to play the public role. On becoming Rochester's wife, donning the ceremonial garb and entering the state of matrimony, Jane is adopting a public role somewhat at odds with her private personality.

The looking-glass allows Jane to see into herself. When as a young child she is incarcerated in the dreaded red room in the Reed's house, she sees her image reflected in the looking-glass:

> All looked colder and darker in that visionary hollow than in reality: and the strange little figure there gazing at me, with a white face and arm specking the gloom, and glittering eyes of fear moving where all else was still, had the effect of a real spirit: I thought it like one of the tiny phantoms, half fairy, half imp . . . coming up out of lone, ferny dells in moors. (17.20-27)

Jane's environment, like that provided for the adventures of Lewis Carroll's Alice *Through the Looking Glass* (1872), juxtaposes two domains separated by the threshold device of a mirror. Take but one step through the looking glass and strange metamorphoses take place. Masks of politeness disappear. Guilty desires can be openly confronted. Rochester's dwelling, Thornfield Hall, is depicted as an enchanted castle made up of fire and ice, glassworks and reflected light, with "large mirrors" which repeat the blending of "snow and fire" (204.18-19). Rochester, himself, like the reflecting surface of a mirror, is for Jane the threshold between two domains: maid versus wife, repression versus emotional fulfillment, sterility versus motherhood.

Reflective surfaces in narrative can be figurative as well as literal. Not all mirrors are made of glass. Lover's eyes, for example, create an image of the beloved. Often the lover's image of the beloved differs strikingly from that imagined by the reader of the text. Kurtz's Intended Bride reflects an image of Kurtz quite different from that formed by Marlow. She, of course, has not experienced the illuminating vision through the field glasses which shows to Marlow the human heads decorating the innermost dwelling of her betrothed in Africa (HD 130-31).

The conclusion of "Heart of Darkness" creates a strong dramatic irony in that the real reader has a vision of Kurtz different from that of his Intended Bride. The text thwarts narrative closure in part because the audience and the characters on stage do not reach a communal agreement or common understanding about the character of Kurtz. The Intended Bride's delusion in "Heart of Darkness" differs from Othello's delusion in Shakespeare's play because Othello and the audience have the same *perception* of the handkerchief in Cassio's hand, but draw differing *inferences* about what they see. In "Heart of Darkness" only Marlow sees the severed heads on stakes through his glasses. Only Marlow perceives the evidence of Kurtz's crime. Lacking ocular proof to the contrary, the Intended Bride remains faithful to her delusion about Kurtz.

The Intended Bride of Kurtz maintains a constant, unchanging image of her beloved. In *Wide Sargasso Sea*, however, Antoinette's reflection in her lover's eye is inconstant. At first Rochester is enchanted by her exotic beauty. Under the influence of the denunciations by Daniel Cosway and the side effects of Christophine's poisonous love potion, Rochester, like Othello, begins to change his image of the beautiful young wife. He changes her name from elegant "Antoinette" to the ugly sounding "Bertha":

> "My name is not Bertha; why do you call me Bertha?"
> "Because it is a name I am particularly fond of. I think of you as Bertha."
> (135)

The mis-naming of Antoinette by Rochester indicates a process of mis-appropriation. Rochester and his clan invade and take possession of Antoinette's *propria persona*. The English succeed in stealing Antoinette's soul. They deprive her of her proper name and her self-image and substitute a picture of herself in the mirror at Thornfield Hall which is brutal and degraded.

The lover mirrors the image of the beloved. A faithful lover, like Kurtz's Intended Bride or Lord Jim's Jewel, can maintain the image, constant against all contrary witness. The unfaithful lover, lacking in fidelity to the impression, falls prey to delusion and allows the image to decay and to become tarnished, like Desdemona's Othello or Antoinette's Rochester. True love is blind in this sense, immune to the deception of ocular "proof."

As a mirror holds its image, so the lover holds the picture of the beloved. So, likewise, the community at large or the band of warriors holds the notion of the honor of the hero. Robert Browning's Childe Roland enters the perilous domain, traverses the waste land, comes to the dark tower, and sounds the horn, unlike his failed companions in arms, Cuthbert and Giles, who were faithless in the quest. Such a pattern of the Romance Quest displays a code of heroic conduct. Marlow, in explaining why he interests himself in the "affair" (59.12) of Lord Jim, claims that they are both members of the seafaring "body of men held together by a community of inglorious toil and by fidelity to a certain standard of conduct" (LJ 59.15-17). Marlow investigates Jim's case searching for some excuse for Jim's abandonment of the Patna. Marlow says he must search for some extenuation of Jim's behavior because he can not bear to doubt "the sovereign power enthroned in a fixed standard of conduct" (59.28-29).

When Jim breaks the code of the naval officer and abandons the Patna to save himself, he alienates himself from the values Marlow finds at the center of honor. Jim can never go home again, never cross the threshold from the perilous domain to be respected among friends and peers,

> We return to face our superiors, our kindred, our friends—those whom we obey and those whom we love . . . to meet the spirit that dwells within the land. (271.03-09)

Marlow believes that Jim feels he has been unfaithful to "some such truth or some such illusion" (272.07-08).

For "some such truth or some such illusion," the reader might substitute "some such impression." The basis of honor and the root of love in Conrad is an impression. Fidelity to such impressions, especially in the face of a community which does not share in the vision, creates the role of alien hero whose acts set him or her apart from the ordinary crowd and generate pity and fear in the audience. The whole shape of Conrad's personal life was the consequence of his father's fidelity to a romantic illusion of Polish independence, which led Apollo Korzeniowski (1820-69) to become involved in the foolhardy 1863 insurrection of Poland against Czarist Russia. Like Browning's Childe Roland, Apollo Korzeniowski was faithful to his quest, dauntless in his defiant challenge to the dark tower. His son had many years to contemplate the consequences of his father's unshaken fidelity to such a romanticized ideal. Does fidelity to an illusion make the protagonist a hero or a fool?

Persistence in a set of motives or attitudes is what makes a sense of self-identity possible. Hume, in *Section VI: Of Personal Identity* in Book I of *A Treatise of Human Nature*, maintains that the notion of *self* is

> Nothing but a bundle or collection of different perceptions, which succeed each other with an inconceivable rapidity, and are in perpetual flux and movement. Our eyes cannot turn in their sockets without varying our perceptions. Our

thought is still more variable than our sight . . . The mind is a kind of theatre, where several perceptions successively make their appearance; pass, repass, glide away, and mingle in an infinite variety of postures and situations . . . (321-22)

For Hume self-identity is an illusion produced by striving for some consistent end, as a ship might have over the years every part in it replaced and renewed, yet still be considered the identical ship as at its outset because its parts all combine toward a persistent, common end. Fidelity to an end creates the illusion of identity.

The framed tales of "Heart of Darkness" or *Lord Jim* provide the impressionist theater "where several perceptions successively make their appearance; pass, repass, glide away, and mingle in an infinite variety of postures and situations" before the eyes of Marlow. In that theater, certain characters like Lord Jim have the opportunity to remain faithful to their illusions or to abandon their beliefs. If Jim violates his illusion of the duties of a British naval officer and abandons the Patna's helpless passengers, he destroys his self-identity. He no longer is what he superficially seems to be. On the other hand, if he suicidally appears unarmed before the father of Dain Waris, to take the guilt for Dain's death on his own head, his fidelity to his code of conduct creates his heroic identity, even as his life is taken from him.

Ford Madox Ford bears the name of one of the major Pre-Raphaelite artists, his maternal grandfather Ford Madox Brown (1821-93), and Ford as a child knew the painter Dante Gabriel Rossetti (1828-82) and his artistic circle, but Ford himself had no formal training as an artist. Conrad and Rhys, too, were not educated to draw or paint. Among the central group of writers here under discussion, only Charlotte Brontë had lessons in drawing and aspired to be a painter. Christine Alexander and Jane Sellars, in *The Art of the Brontës*, catalogue all of her existing paintings and drawings and place them in the context of her life and education. Although Charlotte Brontë plainly has a strong visual imagination, the kind of art education she received, the practice of copying closely the conventions of previous artists, was perhaps damaging to her artistic development. It is possible that the exercises in copying and the method of teaching she experienced restricted her artistic vision to conventional imitation, so that she turned to story telling as a way to liberate herself from the limitations of pictorial representation through her verbal narrative.

Among Charlotte Brontë's earliest juvenile paintings are her miniature illustrations of characters and scenes depicting the imaginative worlds created by the Brontë children for their Angria and Glass Town sagas. From these childhood works, Charlotte Brontë progresses to the creation of "fancy pieces," ornamental genre scenes, which were generally considered appropriate at that time for a young woman with artistic inclinations. Her "Boy and his Dog," for example, depicts a young boy in skirts riding a St. Bernard which is opening a gate with its paw. The cloying sweetness of the composition provides practice in line drawing for the elementary student of art, but does not bode well for the development of honest and sharp expression of the personal vision of the young artist. Charlotte Brontë practiced drawing by copying romantic landscapes and dramatic scenes from engravings.

Thomas Bewick's *A History of British Birds* provided the Brontë children with a number of engravings which they copied in pencil or watercolor, for example Charlotte Brontë's "The Mountain Sparrow." She also made numerous drawings of plants and flowers from life, as well as studies of heads and portraits. The scope of her subjects is rather limited and usually reflects the sentimental or romantic cliches common to the engravings she used as models. Her formal education in art involved mainly imitation of the conventions of previous artists, learning to see with the eye of tradition, a tradition which modern critics generally deplore. There is little sense of her personal vision, of capturing or liberating a unique experience, in her watercolors and drawings.

In the opening pages of *Jane Eyre*, Jane is first introduced reading a picture book on a rainy afternoon, in fact it is *Bewick's History of British Birds*, the very book used by the Brontë children as a model for many of their artistic copies (JE 3.18). Jane finds "strangely impressive" (4.18) a series of pictures in *Bewick's History of British Birds* of seascapes in arctic regions, remarkable for the loneliness and melancholy isolation of vast expanses of "death-white realms" (JE 4.15). Other vignettes which hold Jane's attention depict a solitary rock in a storm at sea, a "broken boat stranded on a desolate coast" (4.23), a "ghastly moon" shining through clouds to a illuminate a nocturnal wreck at sea, a newly risen moon shining on a graveyard, "two ships becalmed on a torpid sea . . . believed to be marine phantoms" (5.05), the Devil "pinning down a thief's pack behind him" (5.07), and a "black, horned thing seated aloof on a rock, surveying a distant crowd surrounding a gallows" (5.10-12). If Charlotte Brontë as a child studied Bewick's illustrations with fascination, her impressions of his pictures seem to be translated into the mind of Jane in the novel.

Jane's memorable pictures from *Bewick's History of British Birds* all display isolation, loss, fear, destruction, vastness sometimes at sea or in frozen wastelands, in short, a collection of the cliches of romantic melancholy and alienation. This is the book which John Reed hurls at Jane's head, severely wounding her, because he claims that the book belongs to him. Nowhere in the collection of pictures remembered by Jane from Bewick's book is there light, joy, pleasure, youth, or bright colors, of the sort often associated with French impressionist art.

Not only the *type* of picture which captures Jane's attention, but the *way* she "reads" the pictures is remarkable. Jane says, "Each picture told a story; mysterious often to my undeveloped understanding and imperfect feelings, yet ever profoundly interesting" (5.13-16). She compares the pictures in Bewick to the tales the maid Bessie sometimes tells. Often, the text of *Jane Eyre* appears to proceed in a similar fashion, beginning with a vignette and then bringing the static scene alive by imagining the story behind what appears visible in the artist's eye. The opening image is often a commonplace romantic scene or portrait, then the imagined tale behind the image explains what is going on. Probably, such was the method of composition for the juvenile tales of the Brontë children. At least, Charlotte describes how her father brought a set of toy soldiers for her brother Branwell, and that the children immediately seized the figures and imagined fictional identities for them. Likewise, for example, the *Origins of Angria* begins with a storm at sea and shipwreck in a scene resembling a combination of several of the pictures Jane Eyre admires in Bewick. The invented story behind the shipwreck reveals that the English sailors have been driven to the strange land of Angria, so the scene slides into a narrative of adventure. The picture is like a window opening onto the imaginative world.

When a character is introduced in *Jane Eyre*, often the author gives us first a portrait of the visible exterior, then brings the character to life in action to show invisible qualities. For example, we first see Miss Temple as if we are looking at her portrait taken by some provincial portrait artist. Miss Temple was:

> Seen now, in broad daylight, she looked tall, fair, and shapely; brown eyes, with benignant light in their irids, and a fine pencilling of long lashes round, relieved the whiteness of her large front; on each of her temples her hair, of a very dark brown, was clustered in round curls, according to the fashion of those times, when neither smooth bands nor long ringlets were in vogue; her dress, also in the mode of the day, was of purple cloth, relieved by a sort of Spanish trimming of black velvet; a gold watch (watches were not so common then as now) shone at her girdle. Let the reader add *to complete the picture*, refined features; a complexion, if pale, clear; and a stately air and carriage. (85.23-86.10, emphasis added)

When Jane first meets Rochester, he falls from his horse and she does not know his identity. Yet, his "new face . . . was like a new picture introduced to the gallery of memory; and it was dissimilar to all others hanging there: firstly because it was masculine; and secondly, because it was dark, strong, and stern" (228.25-229.01).

Perhaps Charlotte Brontë came to feel some dissatisfaction with the restrictions of her own artistic education. One of Jane Eyre's most highly developed accomplishments, like Charlotte Brontë's, is to paint and draw. Rochester's growing erotic attraction to Jane is expressed prominently in the scene in which she shows him her portfolio of art works and he responds to her intimate revelations. Jane asserts that her art work differs from the conventional romantic landscapes and sentimental scenes which make up most of Charlotte Brontë's production. Jane's pictures are not copies, she says, but designs drawn from "out of my head" (247.05).

There are three drawings in the portfolio which Jane displays for Rochester. Touchingly, in this scene Jane turns away from her dramatic interaction with Rochester and addresses the reader directly, deprecating her art:

> I will tell you, reader, what they are: and first, I must premise that they are nothing wonderful. The subjects had indeed risen vividly on my mind. As I saw them with the spiritual eye, before I attempted to embody them, they were striking; but my hand would not second my fancy, and in each case it had wrought but a pale portrait of the thing I had conceived. (247.14-21)

At first glance, these sentences appear to be stereotypical feminine self-deprecation. But possibly the apologetic direct address to the reader stems from Charlotte Brontë's real conviction that her art work is not an adequate expression of her imagination and she tries to convey in words here what her watercolors failed to do.

How should the reader react to Jane's portfolio exposed to Rochester's eyes? Some readers will certainly find her pictures unintentionally funny, a pastiche of sentimental cliches, a hodgepodge of all the images remembered from Bewick's vignettes. If Jane's imagination really is limited to this iconographic range, it displays how damaging her education has been. Three watercolors are described in detail. The first is an over-the-top seascape:

> Clouds low and livid, rolling over a swollen sea: all the distance was in eclipse; so, too, was the foreground; or rather, the nearest billows, for there was no land. One gleam of light lifted into relief a half-submerged mast, on which sat a cormorant, dark and large, with wings flecked with foam; its beak held a gold bracelet, set with gems . . . Sinking below the bird and mast, a drowned corpse glanced through the green water; a fair arm was the only limb clearly visible, whence the bracelet had been washed or torn. (247.24-248.10)

The second watercolor is a nocturne depicting the Evening Star:

> For foreground only the dim peak of a hill, with grass and some leaves slanting as if by a breeze. Beyond and above spread an expanse of the sky, dark blue as at twilight: rising into the sky, was a woman's shape to the bust, portrayed in tints as dusk and soft as I could combine. The dim forehead was crowned with a star; the lineaments below were seen as through the suffusion of vapour; the eyes shone dark and wild; the hair streamed shadowy . . . (248.11-21)

The third picture is of an arctic wasteland:

> The pinnacle of an iceberg piercing a polar winter sky: a muster of northern lights reared their dim lances, close serried, along the horizon. Throwing these into distance, rose, in the foreground, a head,——a colossal head, inclining

towards the iceberg, and resting against it. Two thin hands, joined under the forehead, and supporting it, drew up before the lower features a sable veil; a brow quite bloodless, white as bone, and an eye, hollow and fixed, blank of meaning but for the glassiness of despair, alone were visible. Above the temples, amidst wreathed turban folds of black drapery . . . gleamed a ring of white flame, gemmed with sparkles of a more lurid tinge. This pale crescent was 'The Likeness of a Kingly Crown' . . . (248.27-249.16)

How is the reader to respond to these images? Rochester does not give much guidance. He asks Jane if she was happy while painting these pictures, if she labored long at the task, and if she is satisfied with the result. "The drawings are, for a school girl, peculiar," Rochester says (250.15-16). Does Rochester find her art work pathetic, pitiably weak execution, demonstrating the limitations of Jane's mind? Or, is he touched by the loneliness of her situation and the spark of hope glimmering amidst desolation? Do the pictures allow him to enter her mind, to see with her eyes?

Jane had explained earlier in *Jane Eyre* that visual images trigger her imagination, "Each picture told a story; mysterious often to my undeveloped understanding and imperfect feelings, yet ever profoundly interesting" (5.13-16). As Jane tells her tale, she often reduces an episode of the narrative to a striking vignette which cryptically condenses the story to an image. For example, consider the episode in which Jane first lays eyes on Rochester as the black rider, preceded by his great dog, galloping like a ghostly gytrash along the frozen causeway (218 and following); or, again, the great storm at night in which the lightning blasts the ancient horse chestnut tree in the orchard which visually expresses the emotional storm of the first kiss between Jane and Rochester (519 and following); or, yet again, the extremely powerful visualization of Jane's humiliation and disappointment in the wedding scene in which the ceremony is interrupted by the revelation that Rochester is concealing his mad wife, beginning with these words:

> And now I can recall the picture of the gray old house of God rising calm before me, of a rook wheeling round the steeple, of a ruddy morning sky beyond, I remember something, too, of the green grave mounds; and I have not forgotten, either, two figures of strangers, straying amongst the low hillocks . . . (588.07-13)

The picture comes to life. Its sinister elements foreshadow events. The emotion it evokes requires an explanatory story. The strangers lurking among the graves, of course, bring the denunciation of Rochester's planned bigamy.

Pictorial images trigger the narrative, as if the audience was strolling through a picture gallery or leafing through a book of prints and imagining a story behind each representation. An examination of the denominated concept "picture" in Ford's *The Good Soldier* indicates that Ford follows the same practice as

Brontë, bringing to life in words a visual representation and condensing the story into a few visual features. Dowell speaks of the situation of his unfaithful wife, Florence, who sees Edward Ashburnham's interest shift from herself to the girlish Nancy Rufford:

> It is almost too terrible, the *picture* of that judgment, as it appears to me sometimes, at nights. It is probably the suggestion of some *picture* that I have seen somewhere. But upon an immense plain, suspended in mid-air, I seem to see three figures, two of them close in an intense embrace, and one intolerably solitary. It is in black and white, my *picture* of that judgment, an etching perhaps, perhaps; only I cannot tell an etching from a photographic reproduction. And the immense plain is the hand of God, stretching out for miles and miles, with great spaces above it and below it. And they are in the sight of God, and it is Florence that is alone . . . (78.15-27, emphasis added)

When Ford's *The Good Soldier* was reprinted by Vintage Books in 1957 in the volume with a prefatory "An Interpretation" by Mark Schorer, which sparked the modern revival of interest in Ford, the cover design by Stephen Greene for the paperback edition depicted the haunting love triangle in a desolate black and white plain described by Ford's text. For many readers, this single visual image of erotic alienation encapsulates the condensed essence of Dowell's tale. Later, in real life, this cruel triangle was played out by Stella Bowen and Ford, with Rhys as the outcast. The image is a displacement of feelings of guilt and pity arising from erotic exclusion. The picture and the text of Dowell's story about Leonora, Edward, and Florence might disguise and adumbrate biographical events too painful to face directly. Both picture and text are a way to avert the eyes from an unbearable truth.

Most of Dowell's story in Ford's *The Good Soldier* can be imagined in a series of vignettes making up a gallery of pictures. In addition to the guilty love triangle discussed above, consider the scene in which Florence discovers that her mask of respectability is about to be stripped away and that Edward is transferring his affection from her to Nancy. When she sees Edward and Nancy together in the dark, she is on the verge of her suicide. Dowell develops this story from this image:

> There you have the *picture*, the immensely tall trees, elms most of them, towering and feathering away up into the black mistiness that trees seem to gather about them at night; the silhouettes of those two upon the seat; the beams of light coming from the Casino, the woman all in black peeping with fear behind the tree-trunk. It is melodrama . . . (127.04-10, emphasis added)

At each climax in the story, the narrative explodes from a visual, condensed image. For example, when Nancy finally realizes that Edward is dying of love for her:

> You have to imagine horrible *pictures* of gloom and half lights, and emotions
> running through silent nights—through whole nights. You have to imagine my
> beautiful Nancy appearing suddenly to Edward, rising up at the foot of his bed,
> with her long hair falling, like a split cone of shadow, in the glimmer of a
> night-light that burned beside him . . . like a spectre, suddenly offering herself
> to him . . . (278.23-279.01, emphasis added)

Later we see this picture again as Dowell tells us that:

> The *picture* . . . never left his imagination—the girl, in the dim light, rising up
> at the foot of his bed. He said that it seemed to have a greenish sort of effect
> as if there were a greenish tinge in the shadows of the tall bedposts that framed
> her body. (274.05-09, emphasis added)

The "shadows of the tall bedposts" frame Nancy's virginal body. The whole
story explodes from that image, much as the story of Conrad's "Heart of
Darkness" explodes through Marlow's binoculars as he brings into focus the
image of the smiling, severed, black head decorating the place where Kurtz
dwells.

When Ford denominates the word "picture" in *The Good Soldier*, more often
than not, he explicitly refers to a visual image, usually a dramatized scene, which
is a dreamlike condensation encapsulating a chunk of the plot. These "pictures"
might be considered shadows of the plot. Sometimes the images foreshadow
events to come, in other cases the image is a "side-show," indicating something
that might have happened, but did not, like a forking path not taken in some
labyrinth constructed by Jorge Luis Borges or like the rejected alternative, so
characteristic of the romance in Nathaniel Hawthorne's work. Recall the opening
chapter of Hawthorne's *The Scarlet Letter*, "The Prison Door," in which there
is depicted a blooming rose bush beside the grim portal to the prison. The text
tells the reader that there are two conflicting explanations for the existence of the
rose bush: either it is a remnant left after the New England settlers cleared the
primal wilderness, or it miraculously sprang up from the footsteps of the sainted
Anne Hutchinson when she entered that prison. The storyteller places side by
side the two shadows and forces the reader to choose between the alternatives.
Maintaining the miraculous possibility in the midst of grim reality injects the
sense of wonder and mystery into Hawthorne's romance.

Condensed dreamlike pictures which encapsulate, foreshadow, and side
shadow are a characteristic feature of Ford's Tietjens tetralogy, *Parade's End*.
Like a viewer in a museum of modern art, the reader spirals into the text by
passing in front of a series of pictorial images.

The opening paragraph of the first volume in *Parade's End*, *Some do
not . . .* , presents a dramatized visual scene. Two young men, later identified
as Christopher Tietjens and Macmaster, are traveling in a perfectly appointed,
smoothly working English train, but down what a forking path in the labyrinth

of history are they unwittingly going toward the trenches of World War I. Little
do these heroes know what threshold they are crossing, into what ominous tract
they are entering all unaware:

> The two young men—they were of the English public official class—sat in the
> perfectly appointed railway carriage. The leather straps to the windows were
> of virgin newness; the mirrors beneath the new luggage racks immaculate as if
> they had reflected very little; the bulging upholstery in its luxuriant, regulated
> curves was scarlet and yellow in an intricate, minute dragon pattern, the design
> of a geometrician in Cologne. The compartment smelt faintly, hygienically of
> admirable varnish; the train ran as smoothly—Tietjens remembered thinking—
> as British gilt-edged securities. It travelled fast . . .   (PE 3)

The superficial order and excellent design of this railway machine is conveying
Tietjens rapidly toward, as yet, unimagined torment and suffering. The design
of a geometrician in Germany is barely visible imprinted on the proud British
manufacture. The mirrors have, as yet, seen very little. With hindsight the
reader sees this perfectly appointed train to Hell as a condensed image of the
British Empire in the years just before World War I.

In reality the waste land between the trenches in World War I is an expression,
a rendering accessible to the senses, of the spiritual bankruptcy of the modern
world. The fertile fields of northern France become the poisonous, blighted
no man's land between the front lines. Ford begins the second book of the
Tietjens's tetralogy, *No More Parades*, with a nocturne in the trenches under
bombardment.

> When you came in the space was desultory, rectangular, warm after the drip
> of winter night, and transfused with a brown-orange dust that was light. It was
> shaped like a house a child draws. Three groups of brown limbs spotted with
> brass took dim high-lights from shafts that came from a bucket pierced with
> holes, filled with incandescent coke and covered in with a sheet of iron in the
> shape of a funnel. Two men . . . crouched on the floor beside the brazier . . . "
> (PE 291)

This static scene comes to life as the German barrage zeros in, "An immense
tea-tray, its voice filling the black circle of the horizon, thundered to the ground"
(PE 291). The ultimate destination of the well-oiled British railway train lies
here in the trenches where tea trays disintegrate.

Corresponding to Ford's image of trench warfare in his Tietjens's tetralogy is
the fire at Thornfield Hall, the blinding of Rochester which opens his eyes, in
Charlotte Brontë's *Jane Eyre*. The emotional confusion and frustration of the
characters becomes shadowed forth in the massive destruction and disintegration
of Rochester's ancestral home. It seems that Charlotte Brontë averts her eyes
from that conflagration and cannot bear to let Jane see it directly. Jane, of
course, is far from Thornfield Hall when it burns and she does not know of

the catastrophe when she approaches her former residence. As she is about to
see Rochester's home, her imagination constructs a fanciful picture, so that Jane
creates a side shadow of the event, rather than a direct depiction of it.

> A lover finds his mistress asleep on a mossy bank; he wishes to catch a glimpse
> of her fair face without waking her. He steals softly over the grass, careful
> to make no sound; he pauses—fancying she has stirred: he withdraws; not
> for worlds would he be seen. All is still: he again advances: he bends above
> her; now his eyes anticipate the vision of beauty . . . How he starts! How he
> suddenly and vehemently clasps in both arms the form he dared not, a moment
> since, touch with his finger . . . He thought his love slept sweetly; he finds she
> is stone-dead. (JE 858.05-23)

This visualization of the dead beloved discovered by the lover is what Jane
Eyre substitutes for her eyewitness of the fire at Thornfield Hall. As the lover
approaches his dead beloved, imagining her asleep, so Jane approaches the hall,
"I *looked* with timorous joy towards a stately house; I *saw* a blackened ruin" (JE
858.24-25). The actual event comes to Jane as told by a garrulous, old butler (JE
560.23-868.09). Jane does not see the fire for herself, nor does she formulate a
visual image of it. Jean Rhys bores in on Charlotte Brontë's aversion. Who can
look directly into the fire? Whose mental state is most nearly expressed by the
flames? Where is the picture missing from Charlotte Brontë's *Jane Eyre*? At
the conclusion of Rhys's *Wide Sargasso Sea* the reader is locked into the limited
narration of Antoinette. Since she dies in the fire at Thornfield Hall, Rhys
cannot plausibly have Antoinette describe the conflagration after the fact. Rhys
solves this minor technical problem by foreshadowing. She gives us Antoinette's
nightmare dream vision of what is to come,

> I went into the hall again with the tall candle in my hand. It was then that I
> saw her—the ghost. The woman with streaming hair. She was surrounded by
> a gilt frame but I knew her. I dropped the candle I was carrying and it caught
> the end of a tablecloth and I saw flames shoot up. As I ran or perhaps floated
> or flew I called help me Christophine help me and looking behind me I saw
> that I had been helped. There was a wall of fire protecting me but it was too
> hot, it scorched me . . . (188-89)

Antoinette dreams she ascends to the battlements. She imagines the jungle
aflame with blossoms and the death of her pet parrot with its feathers blazing
when the Coulibri estate burned. She imagines her hair streaming in the wind
as she looks down from the enormous height of the roof and Tia taunting
her to jump. Then, she "jumped and woke" (190). This scene of the fire at
Thornfield, as yet, is only Antoinette's dream. In the final paragraph in Rhys's
*Wide Sargasso Sea* Antoinette sets out to enact her vision, to bring her imagined
picture to life.

There are many apparent, perhaps merely accidental or superficial, reasons why Rhys retells the story of the madwoman in Rochester's attic. Like Rochester's mad wife, Rhys was from the West Indies, an alienated female in a hostile British world. As Rochester's love for Antoinette Cosway turned to repulsion and his affection transferred to Jane Eyre, so Rhys was rejected by Ford and Stella Bowen after she had been led to trust them. She played out in real life the role of the fictional alien woman. In rewriting *Jane Eyre* Rhys gave voice to her personal anguish.

Beneath such obvious biographical motives for Rhys to take up the story of the madwoman in the attic, however, are a set of deeper conditions contributing to her artistic success. The power of Rhys's *Wide Sargasso Sea* flows from her development of the program of literary impressionism which she encountered on the Left Bank of Paris through her association with Ford. Meeting Ford made a mess of her life, but a success of her art.

As if she and Ford were competing for the most advanced step in the march of literature, she strides ahead of Ford's Tietjens Tetralogy in the same way that Ford tried to advance beyond the masterpieces which Conrad created while he and Ford collaborated at the turn of this century. The encounter of Ford and Rhys replays the earlier collaboration of Ford and Conrad. In both cases a burst of creative activity and innovation in narrative form accompanies an authentic engagement of the author with the affairs discussed. It helps the reader understand the power of the best fiction by Rhys, Ford, and Conrad to place their works in a sequence or series, the impressionist *March* in Ford's phrase, *The March of Literature from Confucius to Modern Times*. The series might be composed of Charlotte Brontë's *Jane Eyre*, Robert Browning's *The Ring and the Book*, Flaubert's *Madame Bovary*, Maupassant's *Fort comme la mort*, James's *The Turn of the Screw*, followed by Conrad's *Lord Jim* and "Heart of Darkness," Ford's *The Good Soldier* and his Tietjens Tetralogy, and Rhys's fiction capped by *Wide Sargasso Sea*. Little noticed, one of the most compelling innovations of French Impressionist painting in the years leading up to World War I is the new manner in which works of art are displayed, merchandised, and consumed by the public. Ford's idea of *The March of Literature from Confucius to Modern Times*, like the structure of modern university courses to study English Literature, depends on the serialization of individual artifacts. Such a strategy of presentation rewards novelty, demands that the artist make it new, and always points to the missing final step in the sequence. As a way to present literature to the consumer, it casts early works in the shadows and highlights the modern and innovative. Clearly, Ford invented his idea of literary impressionism on the march so as to claim the vanguard for himself and his associates and to push to the rear writers who had previously succeeded in selling their now outdated "nuvvles" to the reading public. Ford's *March of Literature from Confucius to Modern Times* presupposes a literary *avant-garde*.

The impressionist method of serial display invites the audience to fill in the gaps, to construct the connections, between the items in the series. When the text of Rhys's *Wide Sargasso Sea* stands next to Charlotte Brontë's *Jane Eyre*, the reader must construct the connecting links between the two separate works. Rhys's text, when juxtaposed to Charlotte Brontë's, calls into play the principles of verbal collage: fragmentation, defamiliarization, juxtaposition, and incrementation requiring an authentic participation of the audience in the construction of the experience of encountering the artifact.

When Rhys attaches *Wide Sargasso Sea* to Charlotte Brontë's *Jane Eyre*, she cuts out fragments from Charlotte Brontë's text, defamiliarizes them by supplying new and unexpected cognitive frames for the sections she has torn out of context. When Rhys juxtaposes the fragmentary scenes quoted from Charlotte Brontë's text with newly invented material, she creates a new design and thus increments the meaning of her quoted passages. Like the anti-war poster which makes a collage by superimposing a picture of an industrial assembly line over that of a burning Asian baby, Rhys's story of Antoinette Cosway juxtaposed with Charlotte Brontë's tale of Jane Eyre creates in the mind of each reader an incremented meaning far greater than that of Antoinette and of Jane considered separately.

The reader, mentally bringing together the texts of *Wide Sargasso Sea* and *Jane Eyre*, senses the collage at work, the incrementation of meaning and the authentic involvement of the audience in the experience of the artifact. Since both texts are told through the limited intelligence of the characters, they mount the psychological reaction of an observer onto the spectacle of the affair. The reader feels the intellectual tension created when *Wide Sargasso Sea* questions the authority of Jane Eyre's voice. Rhys forces the reader to take a critical stance and question the assumptions and judgments which Jane and Rochester project concerning the dark wife. If we see only through the eyes of Jane Eyre, is the ocular proof trustworthy? Once we are locked in the solipsistic mind of the limited, eccentric, unreliable observer, certainty is so elusive that even space and time bend crazily. Ford suggests in his fiction and critical writings that the idea of "literary impressionism" offers a coherent explanation rooted in the thought of Locke, Hume, Comte, Zola, Flaubert, Bergson, Cezanne, and Seurat for the augmented power Rhys creates in her revision, her revisioning, of *Jane Eyre*. By destroying the reader's confidence in the reliability of the narrator, Rhys creates a perilous domain for the reader entering the text, like the hero of romance entering an enchanted forest. Comfortable landmarks disappear. Guidelines trick the eye and things are not what they seem. Perhaps, Ford might say that Rhys follows impressionist methods when she suppresses the author, along with the center of authority, in her text so as to demand an authentic involvement of the reader in experiencing the work. But, then, who dares trust Ford's word?

# BIBLIOGRAPHY

Alexander, Christine, and Sellars, Jane. *The Art of the Brontës*. Cambridge: Cambridge University Press, 1995.

Anonymous. *Sir Gawain and the Green Knight*. Edited by Israel Gollancz. London: Early English Text Society, 1940.

Barth, John. *The Sot-weed Factor*. New York: Grosset and Dunlap, 1960.

Baudelaire, Charles. *Fleurs du mal*. Paris: Garnier, 1957.

Bennett, Arnold. *The Journals of Arnold Bennett*. London: Cassell and Company, Ltd., 1932.

————. *The Old Wives' Tale*. New York: The Modern Library, 1935.

Bergson, Henri. *Essai sur les données immédiates de la conscience*. Geneva: A. Skira, 1945. [*Time and Free Will*. Translated by F. L. Pogson. New York: Harper Torchbooks, 1960.]

————. *Le Rire*. Paris: Presses Universitaires de France, 1975.

Bernard, Claude. *Introduction à l'étude de la médecine expérimental*. Paris: Bailliere, 1865.

Bewick, Thomas. *A History of British Birds,* vol. 1: *Containing the History and Description of Land Birds*; vol. 2: *Containing the History and Description of Water Birds*. Newcastle: T. Bewick; London: Longman & Co., 1816.

Blanc, Charles. *Grammaire des arts du dessin*. Paris: Librairie Renouard, 1882.

Brontë, Charlotte. *Jane Eyre. An Autobiography Edited by Currer Bell*. London: Smith, Elder, and Company, 1847.

————. *A Concordance to Charlotte Brontë's Jane Eyre*. Edited by C. Ruth Sabol and Todd K. Bender. New York: Garland Publishing, Inc., 1981.

Brontë, Emily. *Wuthering Heights*. London: Thomas Cautley Newby, 1847.

Browning, Robert. *The Poetical Works of Robert Browning*. London: Oxford University Press, 1960.

————. *The Ring and the Book*. New York: W. W. Norton and Company, Inc., 1961.

Carroll, Lewis. *Alice's Adventures in Wonderland and Through the Looking Glass*. New York: New American Library, 1960.

Cervantes, Miguel de. *The Adventures of Don Quixote de la Mancha*. New York: Farrar, Straus, Giroux, 1986.

Comte, Auguste. *Cours de philosophie positive*. Paris: Au Siège de la Société Positiviste, 1892—94.

Conrad, Joseph. *Collected Edition of the Works of Joseph Conrad*. London: Dent, 1946—55.

————. *A Concordance to Conrad's "Heart of Darkness."* Edited by Todd K. Bender. New York: Garland Publishing, Inc., 1979.

———. *A Concordance to Conrad's Lord Jim*. Edited by James W. Parins, Robert J. Dilligan, and Todd K. Bender. New York: Garland Publishing, Inc., 1976.

———. *A Concordance to Conrad's The Mirror of the Sea and The Inheritors*. Edited by Todd K. Bender. New York: Garland Publishing, Inc., 1983.

———. *A Concordance to Conrad's Nostromo*. Edited by James W. Parins, Robert J. Dilligan, and Todd K. Bender. New York: Garland Publishing, Inc., 1984.

———. *A Concordance to Conrad's Under Western Eyes*. Edited by David Leon Higdon and Todd K. Bender. New York: Garland Publishing, Inc., 1983.

Coover, Robert. *The Public Burning*. New York: The Viking Press, 1977.

———. *Pricksongs and Descants*. New York: New American Library, 1969.

Dante Alighieri. *La Divina Commedia*. Milano: Mondadori, 1991.

Darwin, Charles. *The Voyage of the Beagle*. New York: Doubleday & Company, 1962.

Dos Passos, John. *U.S.A.* New York: Harcourt, Brace and Company, 1932.

Dostoyevsky, Fyodor. *Notes from Underground*. Translated by Constance Garnett. New York: The Heritage Press, 1967.

Eliot, T. S. *The Complete Poems and Plays*. New York: Harcourt, Brace and Company, 1952.

Erikson, Erik H. *Childhood and Society*. New York: W.W. Norton and Company, Inc., 1950.

Faulkner, William. *The Sound and the Fury* and *As I Lay Dying*. New York: The Modern Library, 1946.

Fielding, Henry. *History of the Adventures of Joseph Andrews*. Boston: Houghton Mifflin, 1961.

Flaubert, Gustave. *Madame Bovary*. Paris: Garnier, 1961.

Ford, Ford Madox. *The Inheritors* [with Joseph Conrad]. London: William Heinemann, 1901.

———. *Romance* [with Joseph Conrad]. London: Smith Elder, 1903.

———. *The Fifth Queen*. London: Alston Rivers, 1906.

———. *Privy Seal*. London: Alston Rivers, 1907.

———. *The Fifth Queen Crowned*. London: Eveleigh Nash, 1908.

———. *The Good Soldier*. Edited by Mark Schorer. New York: Vintage Books, 1960.

———. *Concordance to Ford Madox Ford's The Good Soldier*. Edited by C. Ruth Sabol and Todd K. Bender. New York: Garland Publishing, Inc., 1981.

———. *On Heaven*. London: John Lane, 1918.

———. *Joseph Conrad: A Personal Remembrance*. London: Duckworth, 1924.

———. *The March of Literature from Confucius to Modern Times*. London: George Allen and Unwin, Ltd., 1938.

———. *Parade's End*. New York: Vintage Books, 1979. [The Tietjens Tetralogy composed of *Some Do Not . . .* (1924), *No More Parades* (1925), *A Man Could Stand Up* (1926), and *Last Post* (1928).]

Fraser, George Macdonald. *Flashman*. New York: World Publishing Company, 1969.

Goffman, Erving. *The Presentation of Self in Everyday Life*. New York: Doubleday & Company, 1959.

Hawthorne, Nathaniel. *The Scarlet Letter*. Edited by Sculley Bradley, Richard Croom Beatty, E. Hudson Long, and Seymour Gross. New York: W. W. Norton and Company, Inc., 1978.

Helmholtz, Hermann Ludwig Ferdinand von. Edited by Morris Kline. *Popular Scientific Lectures*. New York: Dover Publications, Inc., 1962. [Includes translations of "The Relation of Optics to Painting," "Harmony in Music," and "Recent Progress in the Theory of Vision."]

Hemingway, Ernest. *A Farewell to Arms*. New York: Scribner's, 1929.

Homer, William Innes. *Seurat and the Science of Painting*. Cambridge: The M. I. T. Press, 1964.

Hughes, Thomas. *Tom Brown's Schooldays*. Oxford: Oxford University Press, 1989.

Hume, David. *The Philosophical Works of David Hume*. London: Adam Black, William Tait, and Charles Tait, 1826. [Vol. I contains *Inquiry Concerning Human Understanding*.]

Huxley, Aldous. *Brave New World*. London: Chatto and Windus, 1932.

James, Henry. *The Novels and Tales*. New York: Scribner's, 1907—09.

Locke, John. *An Essay Concerning Human Understanding*. Edited by Peter H. Nidditch. Oxford: Clarendon Press, 1975.

Maupassant, Guy de. *Romans: Une Vie, Bel-ami, Mont-Oriol, Pierre et Jean, Fort comme la mort, Notre Coeur*. Edited by Louis Forestier. Paris: Editions Gallimard, 1987.

Mitchell, Margaret. *Gone With the Wind*. New York: Macmillan, 1936.

Orwell, George. *1984*. London: Secker & Warburg, 1949.

Pater, Walter. *The Renaissance*. London: Macmillan, 1907.

Poe, Edgar Allen. *Complete Stories and Poems*. New York: Doubleday, 1966.

Pynchon, Thomas. *Gravity's Rainbow*. New York. The Viking Press, 1973.

Rhys, Jean. *The Left Bank* [Preface by Ford Madox Ford]. London: Jonathan Cape, 1927.

———. *Quartet*. New York: Vintage Books, 1974. [So titled in 1929, originally published as *Postures*.]

———. *After Leaving Mr. Mackenzie*. London: Jonathan Cape, 1931.

———. *Good Morning, Midnight*. London: Constable, 1930.

———. *Voyage in the Dark*. London: Constable, 1934.

———. *Wide Sargasso Sea*. New York: W. W. Norton & Company Inc., 1982. [First published London: Andre Deutsch, 1966.]

———. *Tigers Are Better-Looking*. London: Andre Deutsch, 1968.

Rood, Ogden N. *Modern Chromatics*. New York: Van Nostrand Reinhold, 1973.

Roy, Jules. *Les Chevaux du soleil*. Paris: Bernard Grasset, 1980.

Stevens, Wallace. *The Collected Poems of Wallace Stevens*. New York: Alfred A. Knopf, 1955.

Swift, Jonathan. *Gulliver's Travels and Other Writings*. New York: The Modern Library, 1958.

Taine, Hippolyte. *Voyage en Italie*. Paris: Librarie Hachette, 1901—02.

Tolstoy, Leo. *War and Peace*. New York: Penguin, 1982.

Watt, Ian. *Conrad in the Nineteenth Century*. Berkeley: University of California Press, 1979.

White, T. H. *Mistress Masham's Repose*. London: Jonathan Cape, 1947.

Webster, John. *The White Devil*. London: Methuen, 1986.

Zamyatin, Yevgeni Ivanovich. *We*. New York: Viking Press, 1972. [First published 1924.]

Zola, Emile. *Le roman experimental*. Paris: Charpentier et Fasquelle, 1894.

———. *Les Rougon-Macquart: Histoire naturelle et sociale d'une famille sous le second Empire*. Paris: Bibliothèque de la Pléiade, 1964.

# INDEX

Todd K. Bender is Professor of English at the University of Wisconsin—Madison. He earned his Ph.D. at Stanford University, the Diplôme d'Études Françaises at the Université de Nancy II (France), and his B.A. from Kenyon College. Professor Bender has held Fulbright Scholarships three times (to England, Greece, and France), as well as post-doctoral grants from the American Council of Learned Societies (Paris and Oxford). A specialist in Nineteenth Century European literature with an interest in computer applications to literary research, he is the author of *Gerard Manley Hopkins: The Classical Background and Critical Reception of his Work*, The Johns Hopkins Press, 1966, as well as a series of concordances to the complete works of Conrad, Ford Madox Ford's *The Good Soldier*, Charlotte Brontë's *Jane Eyre*, the poems and sermons of Hopkins, and the poems of Keats. He has been member of the Executive Council of The Joseph Conrad Society of America, Chair of the Executive Committee of the Division on Methods of Literary Research of the Modern Language Association, and member of the Board of Scholars of the International Hopkins Association. Professor Bender is also editor of the Origins of Modernism series in the Garland Studies in British Literature.